A]

ADVENTURE TALES

TALL AND TRUE

VERNON (Vern) NOWELL

ALASKAN ADVENTURE TALES, TALL & TRUE

First Edition 2012

Printed in the United States of America by Instantpublisher.com

ISBN: 978-0-578-10657-1

AUTHOR AND PUBLISHER:

Vernon L Nowell
PO Box 7062
Nikiski, AK 99635

e-mail: ponywagon@gci.net

Many of the names have been changed to "Protect the Innocent and the Guilty", Others have been left to give "Honor To Whom It Is Due".

ACKNOWLEDGEMENTS

First and foremost I must thank God for his hand on me over the years, for keeping the scythe of the "Grim Reaper" at bay, although I knew the "Reaper stood at the ready".

I want to thank my wife Sharon for being a beautiful woman of Integrity, who has loved and stood by me over the years, through "Thin Times" and those of "Blessings", who I could always trust, tried to lead our children in a Godly manner, and sacrificed for the horses and airplanes and other expenses used in my never ending quest for Adventure. When flights were overdue she prayed and trusted in God that I was safe and would return, and nursed my wounds when I was wounded.

Thanks to our three wonderful daughters, Laura, Joan, and April, for being the trustworthy, resourceful and loving children who sacrificed when I should have been spending more time with them. I thank you for encouraging me to "write my book" and share the adventures that so many men never realized. I love you three wonderful individuals.

Thanks to our grandchildren who we truly love and wish God's blessings. You don't have to follow the bad choices of the crowd. My Dad used to say "Use your head for something besides a Hat Rack!"

An individual at age eighteen, I left my family and friends in Memphis, TN and ventured to an unknown life of adventure in Alaska, knowing no one or what lay ahead.

Thanks to all my friends who over the years shared or risked their life with me or in the early days "Grubstaked" the venture. Special thanks to Buck, Jay, Doug, Jimmy, and Chuck. Gary thanks for "prodding me to get started on my book"! Thanks Pastor Wayne for including me in your book and encouraging me to share on the written page. Thanks Elsie, your early journals of our lives entwined, refreshed my memory.

I thank my Mother and Father, not perfect, but good parents, for trying to set good examples for my brothers and me. Stern discipline and many chores made me a better person. I hold no resentment nor blame you for my faults and frailties as we each are ultimately responsible for our choices in life. Nor do I begrudge the thousands of miles traveled while visiting and caring for my aging Mother. Had we lived closer, we surely would have visited more.

Thanks Marsy and Lance for the help getting my "Scribbling from our Daniels Lake Cabin" formatted for the printer!

TABLE OF CONTENTS

AN ALASKAN GRIZLY'S REVENGE

The year was 1967 and my Mother and Dad were flying to Anchorage, AK for a visit. I wanted to take my Father on a moose hunt, one that would not be overly strenuous due his history of heart problems, and a heart-attack in the early 1960's, which slowed him down. At that time, the medical world was "backwards" as far as the way to treat the patient. After a heart-attack, you were doomed to the life of a "couch-potato" sitting in front of a television, having someone wait on you, hand-and-foot! You were to do "NO EXERCISE" at all! And this was exactly opposite of what you should do! You needed to get off your fanny and move around, and exercise to re-build your heart and muscles.

My plan was to have my friend Fred Lockwood fly my Father and me to a good hunting location. He was a commercial pilot and big game guide and was also a Union Carpenter with a shortened "trigger-finger" from a saw accident. After the moose was shot, I would do all of the packing to get the meat and antlers to the gravel bar where Fred would fly us back to civilization. The needed gear had been accumulated, for at age eighteen I ventured from Memphis, TN in 1959 to hunt, fish, build a log cabin and live for one year in Alaska, fell in love with Alaska's freedom, the harsh climate and ways, and never returned to the Lower 48, but made the "49th State" my home.

Un-known to me, my Father had other ideas about "flying to a Bush location", as he was more of a "City type hunter" and liked the warmth of a nice cottage or cabin, electric lights, and a cozy fire-place. I later learned, he wanted nothing to do with the small "Bush Plane" and "Roughing It". I remember as a boy when hunting with my dad, all was well, until the sun had done its work and was retiring in the west. At that time of evening, my Dad was usually pointing the automobile towards home, and my Mother's cooking and his warm bed!

I had known Fred since 1960 when he instructed me on how to properly skin and prepare for mounting a Boone and Crockett Trophy Double-Shovel Bull Caribou I had shot and killed with my Ruger Blackhawk .44 Magnum pistol. I was away from my cabin on Bishop Creek, and I had borrowed a .300 Holland and Holland Magnum rifle for the hunt, but the scope was "off-of-impact" and I could not accurately shoot with it. The rifle was returned to the truck and I went out and shot three caribou with my Ruger Blackhawk pistol, one bull scored high enough to go into the Boone and Crocket Club Records.

I had flown with Fred in his Piper PA-11 when beaver trapping on the Kenai

Peninsula and he had flown down from the Birchwood air-strip, and spent a few days with my trapping partner Jay and me. The fact I had asked Fred to fly my Father and me into the bush-country, reaffirmed my friendship and my trust in his ability as a Bush-pilot.

Fred had answered my letter requesting him to drop us off on our hunt, and was glad "I had not written him off as a friend", as he and his wife of many years had recently divorced and Fred quickly "re-married" and was flying and guiding out of Copper Center. I was very surprised to learn of the divorce and felt very sorry for his former wife, Mary. We saw and talked to her later, and she was able to pick up the pieces and go on with life, and also re-married.

Fred was a "First-Class Woodsman" and "Marksman" and had grown up in Michigan where he kept the meat-house supplied with deer he shot with a .22 rim-fire rifle. This was not "Sport-Hunting" but hunting to feed the family. For years, Fred used a Remington Game Master, pump action .270 Winchester caliber rifle to back up his brown and grizzly bear hunters, who were usually shooting a .300 Magnum, or a .338 Winchester Magnum or a .375 Holland & Holland Magnum, but most definitely a rifle larger than Fred's .270! Fred had entered a world-record class grizzly in the Boone and Crocket Book of North American Records that he killed with this .270. After much complaining of the hunters Fred was guiding, he went to a larger caliber for "back-up rifle", to pacify them.

My Mother and Father had arrived in Anchorage and we were waiting for Fred to contact us when I received a phone call from my old trapping partner, Jay, who said Fred had died in an airplane crash! As my wife and I did not subscribe to the newspaper so had not seen the article that told of his death.

Wednesday, September 20, 1967 (which is my birthday) the Anchorage Daily Times Newspaper had the following article:

"SEARCHERS HUNT MISSING PILOT

Glennallen (AP)... A search was under way Tuesday for Fred Lockwood of Copper Center.
Lockwood, flying a white with red trim super cub has been missing since Sunday on a flight.

The search is centered in an area bounded by Chitina, the Wrangell Mountains and the Richardson Highway."

Then, two days later, the following article appeared in the Fairbanks Daily News Miner, Friday, September 22, 1967:

11

"THREE MEN DIE

Juneau (AP)…The wreckage of a light plane that vanished Sunday with three men aboard has been found on Long Glacier, 25 miles northeast of Chitina, Alaska, State Troopers reported today.

The bodies of the three men were picked a by a rescue helicopter from Elmendorf Air Force Base.

The dead were identified as Frederick A. Lockwood of Copper Center, 49, the pilot. Leslie D. Hibbs, Colorado Springs, Colo., and Hibbs' father, Ashbley Hibbs, Salida, Colo."

(Ashby G. Hibbs-age 58, Leslie D. Hibbs-31)

Years later, my wife and I, after having dinner at the home of new friends who had ventured up from Colorado to North Kenai, as we were talking, something "triggered" me to tell of Fred and his hunter's accident. When I related this story, the lady said the hunters were good friends of her mother, who now lived in Alaska. It was through this family I learned more of the story: The father and son team had hunted extensively in the lower-48 and the Rockies and owned a Piper Super Cub aircraft, which was

12

said to be offered as the payment of their dream hunt in Alaska. A deal was struck, and as usual, Fred had located and put them on to good trophies and the hunters both collected trophy Dahl sheep, exceptional caribou and their huge bull moose, and were now ready for the grizzly bears!

Sunday, September 17, 1967, the plane was fueled and apparently the men crawled and squirmed their way into the rear of the airplane, and the pilot climbed into the front seat of the Piper Super Cub. I have owned two Super Cubs with the "Third Seat Modification" which consists of "a set of seat-belt mounts installed on the outer-floor area of the baggage section, where a person is allowed sit on the floor and "strap-in", and to ride as long he is not over the weight limit and is properly buckled in. It is a very, very uncomfortable situation, and if you are prone to claustrophobia, you will be guaranteed to lose your mind after a few minutes of riding back there. I am told these were "large men", and not at all skinny, which would help if you were required to sit in that "cubby-hole". I have flown with a two-hundred pound man in the rear seat, and a one-hundred and sixty pound man in the "Third-Seat-Modification" baggage-area. It is very un-stable, and feels like you are dragging an anchor, as if the "tail

section is about to stall" or "fall-out
-of -the-air" due to the excessive aft
weight condition. Very Un-comfortable
flying for me, to say the least! I
always tried to avoid this situation if
at all possible!

We suspect the bear that attracted
their attention was a beautiful Toklat
or "Blonde" or "Golden" grizzly, as
this was the coloration of the bear
that remained at the crash-site
enjoying the ease of locating the
slightly charred meat, and was feasting
on the easy meal provided by my friend
and his hunters! They almost certainly
were flying over the bear in a circle,
trying to judge the trophy, and not
paying enough attention to the
airspeed. This situation is called the
"Moose-Hunter" stall, where the pilot
is lulled into slow flight, usually
just above the stall speed, low
elevation trying to get a better look
at the object or animal on the ground.
If there is a wind in the area, when
the aircraft makes the down-wind turn,
instead of a wind on his nose it
becomes a wind on the tail and the
plane's airspeed drops and the plane
many of the times stalls, enters a spin
downward to the ground, with no hope of
recovery!

When the cub slammed to the
ground, hopefully the three men were
killed instantly, as the engine area
erupted in flames and I can only with

great distress, imagine the horrible, excruciatingly painful and "hell-like-death" in the flames! Whether the bear remained in the area after the crash and began feasting on the charred bodies soon after the fire, I can't say. The bear might have been drawn back to the area by the scent of the charred flesh that permeated the air from the burned bodies in the fuselage. By the time the rescue team located the crash site, the bodies had been pulled from the fuselage and feasted upon, leaving bones scattered over a large area.

The "Rescue Team" from Elmendorf "gathered the bones that remained" and a box about the size of a cardboard beer case with "all of the remains of Fred" was given to his ex-wife Mary.

Years later, I learned the "gathering of the bones by the officials" had been far from thorough, as the guide who was the builder of the Gun-Sight Mountain Lodge, Whitey, landed to check the area after the bodies had been recovered. Whitey said Fred's plane had hit with such force the aluminum prop-spinner had "impact-molded" and formed around the nine-sixteenth inch size bolt-heads, the next size wrench would easily fit over them. Also, the leading-edge of the wings was flattened at a "ninety-degree angle" from the impact, as if a carpenter's square had been used! This

15

indicated the plane impacted straight down with a tremendous force.

Laying next to the aircraft was the now decomposing bullet ridden Toklat Grizzly bear, with its beautiful long blonde hair being pulled away by the magpies and ravens, and scattered by the cold glacier wind. The Super Cub had remained vertical, as a towering monument with the "tail-feathers" (rear section of the aircraft) pointing to the sky, with traces of sun-light rays penetrating the holes it received when the bear was shot while near the wreckage with the barrage of bullets that rained from the helicopter. Whitey gathered the remaining human bones, dug a small trench and buried them.

After the accident, there was a flurry of reports of "sighting of Fred at the Anchorage International Airport", suggesting he had not been in the crash. None of those reports were ever confirmed, so Fred was probably in the wreckage of the Cub. Back then, there was no "DNA test" to prove if the bones matched the person they said they belonged to. I still have a hard time visualizing Fred, with all of his experience, flying and spotting game in the mountains, in a so very much aft-loaded situation.

As stated before, I have flown my Super Cub with the third-passenger that was much lighter in weight than Fred's passenger, and it felt like I was "dragging an anchor"! I also have been in a "stall-spin" type situation where my airplane was totaled and I was injured when I was thrown forward enough to break the compass with my fore-head, and should have been killed. But I survived, only by God's mercy! Although injured and my rifle damaged in the crash, I was still able to shoot and collect the wolverine I was after. That was "A Heck of an Expensive Venture!" The wolverine hangs on the wall as a reminder: the "Twenty-Thousand Dollar Wolverine". (I'll tell you that story later, if you hang around!)

The hunting season in Alaska can be a dangerous time to fly, as in 1967 there had been eighteen reported accidents that month to the National Transportation Safety Board. If that many accidents were reported, there had almost assuredly been a few accidents that were "Not Reported!" Airplane accidents in Alaska are usually reported as a "Last Resort". Very few people want to get a Federal Agency involved if that can be avoided. I later contacted the NTSB to get their report on Fred's accident and it was as follows:

"PA-18A   N6772B
Purpose of flight:
HUNTING

Damage DESTROYED
Type   of   Accident:
STALL: SPIN   3
DEATHS
Probable Cause: PILOT
INCOMMAND- FAILLED TO
MAINTAIN FLYING SPEED
MISSING AIRCRAFT-LATER
RECOVERED
FIRE-AFTER,IMPACT
Pilot-rating:
Commercial
Age, 49,   2088 Total
hours
  REMARKS-   RECOVERY
  DATE 9/21/67"

This ended the lives of three, adventurous hunters, all taken with one sweep of the razor-sharp scythe of the "Grim-Reaper". It was a terrible loss, but each had died doing something they dearly loved, hunting. Would it have been better to have lost them to a slow death battling cancer? Or to some other slow, lingering death? I think not!

HE'S DREAMING. HE'LL NEVER LEAVE HIS HOME IN MEMPHIS!

Working at Southern Metal in 1959, hardly anyone believed I would really leave the safety and comfort of my parent's home and go to some unknown part of the world, not knowing anyone there or how I would survive. There was no one to help me get settled, offer a place to stay and a place to eat, or helping hand when needed. Different ones in high school and friends, and almost anyone I talked to, when told of my plans for an adventurous life, would usually say, "You aren't going anywhere! You're blowing smoke, just dreaming"! I admit I was dreaming, but many of the dreams were to come true!

My original desire was to go to Africa, but that was not looking very good. Graduating in 1958, I had worked at the KKK camp for boys. After spending the summer as assistant nature director at Kamp Kia Kima Boy Scout Camp I found a job at Southern Metal, where my older brother David was working. It was assembly line work, installing springs into window jams, which assisted in the raising of the windows, after installation. It was dry, dusty, and hot work during the summer, fall and spring, and winters were cold in the building. This was a job a hated, but it provided take home pay of $42.00 for a forty hour week. I was living at home and was able to save a good portion of my pay. When I look back now, I regret not helping more with the household expenses of Mother and Dad. Dad told me he would help with my college expense if I would go. But I was consumed with this desire for adventure, and could not think of settling down to four more years of school. I eagerly looked forward to the mailman delivering my issue of "Outdoor Life Magazine", and the first article searched for was written by Jack O'Conner, the Shooting Editor.

With the finances coming in too slow for the trip to Africa, I talked with my school buddy, Jack, and we decided to save our money, buy a Jeep, and drive down through Mexico to Columbia. (At the rate the money was stacking up, I'd be able to apply for Social Security first.) There were jaguar and other cats to hunt, and snakes of all kinds to catch in Columbia. I had read an article where "live anaconda snakes" were selling for $18.00 per foot to pet shops and collectors. While working at the Boy Scout Camp, we "milked pigmy rattlesnakes" and copperhead snakes, and I could visualize making a mint catching and selling those non-poison snakes. My letters to the Columbian Government were returned un-opened. I thought our idea of going to Columbia

was settled, but apparently not, for
when the time to put your money where
your mouth is arrived, Jack backed out
on me. Whether it was the thought of
the snakes, or just leaving the
security of his parent's home, I do not
know. But, I was in a dilemma. What
to do now?

THERE IS WISDOM IN THE
MULTITUDE OF COUNCIL!

An idea came to my mind; why not ask Jack O'Conner, Shooting Editor of Outdoor Life Magazine, and see what he would do, or where he would go, if he were in my boots! So that is exactly what transpired. I fired off a letter to Jack and told him of my situation, and asked for his advice. And "Good Advice" it was. "Vernon", Jack O'Conner wrote, "I would advise you to go to college, get a good education, find yourself a career that pays well, and you can hunt anywhere in the world you want to. Any time you want to." (Although this was advice directed to me, it is still valuable information for anyone getting started in life.)

He also said if you can't wait and do that, "I would advise against going to Africa at this time. There are too many political problems. There is the language problem." During the 1950's the Mau Mau were having an uprising, and were slaughtering many of their own tribesmen that refused to join them, and were raping and butchering white women, children, and men, and toasting, boiling, or barbecuing little white boys like me for dinner! Now that would be a twist to Bobby Fay's cook book, "Boy Meets Grill". Instead of boy meeting the grill and learning how to cook, it would be "Boy Meets Grill

and Gets Cooked!" I would probably end up in the large wood-fired "Crock Pot" but would have been too small for a Friday Night's Bash,
and would have ended up on the "Mau Mau's Monday Morning 'Low Fat' Menu!"

Jack O'Conner advised against South America and recommended Alaska or Canada as the place to go. After sending letters to the Alaskan and Canadian capitols and when receiving and studying the information, being a United States citizen, I decided to go to Alaska. It was three months before my actual departure from Memphis on a "Life-Long Adventure" and required an adjustment from the tropics to the Arctic! They did have one thing in common, Mosquitoes, and lots of them! Most of my gear was ordered from "Klein's of Chicago", a sporting goods and military surplus outlet that advertised in Outdoor Life Magazine.

Another employee at the same plant learned I was going to Alaska alone, and asked if he could join me. Lyalls lived with his Mother and a sister in Memphis. Neither of us came from wealthy families, but I did have it much better. There was also another young college student at work, a son of a local dentist that said he would like to join us. Owning a "Henry J" automobile, he suggested we pool our money to pay for the gasoline, about fifteen cents per gallon at that time, and drive to Alaska. That sounded good to me. By this time I was not as selective as I had been. Talk is cheap, and when it came time to put up or shut up, our driver was too scared to go, and backed out on us. Lyalls and I knew we would have to find a different mode of transportation, and settled on the bus; the one-way fare for two passengers from Memphis to Fairbanks was $314.72. As a side note, Lyalls had to leave Alaska that first November, due to his Mother being diagnosed with cancer, and she died soon after he arrived in Memphis. After Lyalls arrived in Memphis, I received a letter from the dentist's son who backed out on coming to Alaska with us, asking if he could come up and live with me in the log cabin I was building. My answer was "No! If you backed out on me in the beginning when we didn't know what we would be up against, I can't trust you now! You may back out on me if we get into a tight jam or tough times". I usually preferred to go it alone, if I couldn't trust or depend on the person, and still feel that way.

Before writing Jack O'Conner, I had written Patrick Hemmingway, son of Earnest Hemmingway the famous author, who worked as a "White Hunter" in Africa. I did not receive an answer from Patrick Hemmingway until we were building a log cabin with a Swede saw (bow type saw) and axe while living in a canvas wall tent with the ridge pole lashed to a tall standing spruce tree and the front of the pole was supported by an "A" frame. This was erected near Bishop Creek, who's gently flowing water were stained with "tannin" and was the color of tea, was alive at that time of year with native rainbow trout and the spawning salmon, loaded with succulent and nutritious riches of fat and had finally returned home. My Mother and Dad had mailed a "Care Package" as I called them, a box from home that contained my Bandera beaver felt cowboy hat, snacks, cookies, and things of that sort, along with my forwarded mail which included the letter from Earnest Hemmingway's son. Patrick did not mention the college aspect, but reconfirmed what Jack O'Conner had said about Africa and South America. He also suggested going to Alaska or Canada! And that was where I had landed with my second-hand army surplus wall tent pitched about thirty five yards from Bishop Creek, one of the best trout streams on the Kenai Peninsula, Lyalls and I were living the life of adventure!

We ended up moving to the Bishop Creek area where a newly acquired friend, Stan Thompson was proving-up on a "Trade and Manufacturing Site" and needed structures erected. When we first rode to the area, the truck slowly bumped along the cat-trail road, as we topped the hill and looked down at Bishop Creek, there were a few salmon swimming up the rapids, their silvery backs partly exposed in the shallow water of the riffles; it was a conformation to us. Lyalls and I looked at each other, we knew we had arrived! This would be the place we would build our cabin. It was too late in the day to try and set up the wall tent I had purchased from an army surplus store in Memphis, Tennessee, for $15.00. We stretched out a tarp and lay our sleeping bags on top of it, and pulled the tent over us in case of rain. My Custom Springfield .30-06 rifle lay next to me, and during the night the Monarch of Bishop Creek, a huge brown-bear that lived in the area, made his way along the creek, noticed something different, and stopped to get a glimpse of our new camp. He walked around the tent, where we lay sleeping and we were totally unaware of his presence.

The next morning when we got up, we spotted the largest brown bear tracks we were to see for many years. He had completely circled the spot where we slept! We looked at each other and exclaimed that we had arrived! Just knowing we were in the habitat of critters the size of this brown bear raised the "hackle on the back of our neck", and made us feel good!

A Side Note:
Did you see the movie "Lonesome Dove" and the scene where Augustus McCrae returned from rescuing Lori from Blue Duck and the gang? Upon returning to the herd, he said, "Looks like things went to Hell when I left!" I could say the same thing about Memphis!

LIVING A LIFE OF ADVENTURE

September 1, 1978, had been a busy morning! We had stopped along the cold, clear and fast flowing mountain stream, filled my aluminum coffee pot with water and had it hanging over a gently roaring fire made from the sweet smelling willow brush, and we were waiting for the water to boil. Hopefully, this would give the wounded grizzly bear time to either die, or to "stiffen up". Across the creek from us was a pie-shaped patch of alder growing wide at the creek's edge and up the steep hill to form a point at the upper end. In that alder patch was a wounded grizzly bear, waiting for us to come in and try to bring him out! The bear had not started the fight, but might well end it!

The four of us had saddled up and ridden up the narrow valley above camp where my brother David had shot a nice bull moose. As it was too early to end the day's hunting, we had proceeded up the creek a short distance, when a beautiful grizzly bear was spotted. Fall was now upon us and David my older brother from Tennessee had flown up for a free moose hunting trip with me and my hunting partner, Buck, and his friend Dave. The two trucks pulling trailers had transported four horses each and we were parked along the Denali Highway, where Buck landed his

Super Cub airplane on the narrow gravel road.

Later, after a reconnaissance flight to determine the game population, we decided on a likely valley to hunt. We had hunted this area before, and it had produced well for us, giving us numerous trophies and hundreds of pounds of first quality meat for our freezers.

Most of the gear was flown in with the Super Cub, and David, Dave and I rode and trailed the horses across the fast flowing river, up the steep hillside, and along the thick willow and alder brush covered rolling hillside, and finally reached the "Y" in the valley where the two creeks joined and became one. Here we pitched our five-man Army surplus tent and the Eureka six-man tent. From this vantage point, much of the valley could be observed with the tri-pod mounted spotting scope.

Within a short time of leaving camp, we spotted a bull moose and David had emptied his .30-06 rifle, so I quickly handed him my .308 Norma Magnum to complete the job! We had the moose gutted and propped open for cooling in short order, and remounted our horses, and eased our way up the valley. As we rode forward the grizzly was spotted high on the hillside to our right, and it started quartering down the slope toward the creek. Buck quickly loped forward to intercept the grizzly, quickly stopped his horse Joker, and remained on our side of the creek while the bear looked facing him from the other side of the creek. "Shoot him Dave!" Buck called out to his friend, who was getting into position to dispatch the bear with his Custom Pre-64 Model 70 chambered in .300 Weatherby Magnum. I had pulled my rifle from the leather scabbard attached to my saddle, and was standing at the ready. "BOOM!" Dave's rifle roared! The beautiful grizzly was knocked to its side, and was rolling and thrashing in the knee high grass. Thinking the bear was "Down for the Count", I relaxed from my "Port Arms position", when all of a sudden the bear sprang to its feet and was throwing muskeg into the air as it made a dash for the thicket!

The alders were well over a man's height, and too tall to see the bear once it reached the thicket, and only the movement of the tops of the brush gave an indication of the bear's whereabouts as it rushed toward the "point of the pie" up the hill. At one point I got a glimpse of the bear and I quickly fired a round in its direction! Later investigation of the hide revealed my bullet had not connected with him! Buck rode his horse to where we were gathered, and Dave was showing signs of stress! My comment was, "Let's build a fire, have a little lunch and give the bear a chance to either die or stiffen up". So we did!

Now it was time to "Sort Things Out!" Buck and I tightened the cinches of our saddles and rode across the clear creek to inspect the blood trail. I got off my horse and walked to the spot the bear had been rolling about, checked the blood and immediately saw the blood was "too dark" to be a "lung-shot". Blood when an animal has been shot in the lungs will be a "pinkish" color from the oxygen mixed into the blood. Blood from a body wound is more dark red in color. We knew the bear would probably still be in good shape and would be waiting for us to come in after him. There was no doubt we, had a "Fight On Our Hands"!

Buck said, "Vern, let's walk up to the point and ease our way down and get that bear." I said, "No, Buck. Let's not walk up the hill, we'll ride up the hill, tie the horses up there, and then we won't be "winded" when we start in after the bear!" This we agreed on. But now, we needed to get David, my brother, and Buck's friend Dave over to our side of the creek to guard the lower end of the alder patch in case the bear tried to escape from this lower end of the patch. Buck called over to the boys, and told them to come over.

Well, I could have started a fire and baked biscuits in my Dutch Oven within the time it took them to tighten the cinches and finally cross the creek to our side! Dave was saying, "Oh, I didn't want anyone to get hurt because I wounded the bear!" They "Fiddle Farted" around until we had to holler again for them to "Come on over!" Once on our side, we positioned a man with rifle at the ready, at each corner and began our ride up the hill. Once there, we tied the lead ropes and pulled our rifles from the scabbards.

I eased a custom hand-loaded cartridge into the chamber of my .308 Norma Magnum and Buck loaded his Ruger 77 .338 Winchester Magnum. As we started down the right side of the alders, with me about fifteen to twenty feet outside the thicket, Buck walked about fifteen to twenty feet farther out so he would be able to "shoot the bear off me" if need be! You never want to stand too close together in a situation like this, as the bear could get the both of you at the same time! After about forty yards of travel, I was able to pick up a glint of the bear's eyes as it stood watching and waiting for us to come within the kill zone, with only its head exposed in an opening in the foliage! I said, "Hang on, Buck! I see him in the brush!" Buck quickly replied, "Let him have it, Vern!"

I eased my Browning Safari Grade rifle to my shoulder, and placed the cross-hair on the bear's nose, centered between the nostrils, and gently squeezed the trigger. I did not feel the recoil. Only the bear's head had been visible in the small opening of the alders as he stared and waited for us to get within "charging distance". The blonde grizzly dropped from view! I ejected the spent round and placed the empty case in my pocket, to be loaded again at a later date, and chambered a fresh round, and started easing my way to the bear's location. When in a few feet of the alder's edge, I spotted the bear with paws and claws extended and it was still snapping its teeth! I drew my .44 Magnum and gave the grizzly a "Coup de Grace", and motioned for the boys to come up. Dave was so grateful it was all over, and we were thanked for "Sorting It Out" for him. No one had been hurt during this operation. The bear was later tanned and mounted and made into a beautiful trophy for Dave's wall, and with a "Story Waiting to Tell!" As I did not want to destroy the face of the bear for mounting, the bullet entered perfectly centered between the nostrils!

When I left my "Mundane Life in Memphis, Tennessee, in 1959, at the age of eighteen, knowing no one in Alaska, this was the life that awaited me! I have truly been blessed with an Adventurous life!

As a Side Note: I have read that many men dreamed of adventurous things when they were boys, but their dreams never grew to maturity, and problems developed for them in later life. I was just the opposite, and by no means perfect or anywhere close, have been fortunate enough to realize many, many of my "Dreams of Adventure", and at age seventy one, I still live an "Adventurous Lifestyle"! And if I never experienced another adventure, I have been blessed with more than my share!

SUPER CUB IN THE COOK INLET AT THE CHUIT RIVER

It was July 1, 1986, and the king salmon fishing on the west side of Cook Inlet had been slow, but there were hopes of "getting into them!" My wife Sharon's cousin Gary from Minnesota had never landed a king salmon, and Sharon asked if I would take him with me the next time I flew from O'Malley Air Strip to one of our "Secret Fishing Holes" on the west side of Cook Inlet. This I agreed to. When the time arrived, I called and told Gary I would be flying over that evening. He was ready to go!

I tied the fishing poles to the wing struts of the Piper PA-18 Super Cub and loaded our gear into the baggage compartment and did a through pre-flight, we drained our bladders by wetting on the gravel, and Gary climbed into the back seat of the Cub. As usual, I made sure the magneto switch was in the "Off" position. I operated the fuel primer as you would a hypodermic needle, slowly pulling the knob of the fuel primer pump out to load it with gasoline, then pushed it forward with a fast movement to spray fuel into the cylinders. This was done four times to prime each of the four cylinders, I stood behind the prop on the right side of the aircraft and pulled the prop through (rotated the

35

propeller) four strokes, which loaded fuel into each of the four cylinders of the Lycoming one hundred and fifty horse power engine. With the engine primed and ready, I advanced the throttle all the way forward, pulled it back to the rear stop, and then forward about three-quarters of an inch, then I flipped the left magneto to the "On" position and pulled down on the prop, and the engine immediately fired and was running, slightly loping. I reached across the front seat and flipped the right magneto to the "On" position and the engine smoothed, purring like a kitten! There was no need to grind on the started if it is not needed! Climbed into the front seat, slipped the shoulder harness on, and snapped the Heavy-duty Crop-Duster Seat Belt in place. With the door closed, and my David Clark headset with boom microphone adjusted for comfort, I switched the radio on and announced my intentions. With no other aircraft operating in my area I taxied to the end of the runway which gave the engine time to warm and to reach operating temperature, I did a fast run-up while taxing (increase rpm and check each magneto drop and also checked the carburetor heat for proper operation). With everything operating properly I pointed the airplane's nose down the runway and slowly advanced the throttle to the firewall, giving the plane time to roll forward before the engine reached full rpm (with the airplane moving before reaching full rpm, there is less chance of the propeller "sucking up gravel" and putting "nicks" in the propeller's leading-edge). Within a few yards the Super Cub's tail was off the ground and very soon thereafter, I reached my left hand down and pulled the "flap lever" to "Full Flap Position". The little airplane "leaped into the air" and climbed like a "Home-Sick Angel!" Oh My! What a Feeling! If you have never had the opportunity to fly a good PA-18 Super Cub with one-quarter filled fuel tanks and loaded very lightly, you have missed something! It's like the song, "Mount up, on the wings of an Eagle!" I can relate to that song!

With proper clearance from the control tower, we flew through the Anchorage International Airspace, and followed the beach from the Little Susitna River to the Big Susitna, and down the west coast. When we reached the Chuit River, I checked the wind by observing the leaves on the trees, and the waves, and flew low over the trees as we searched the river below for signs of king salmon. There were a few kings spotted, as they lay motionless, appearing like logs under-water. The tide was low enough to expose enough area to land on the sloping beach, and I came in with half flaps, then I pulled full flaps as we settled toward the chosen "Touch-Down Spot". With a slight nose-high position, the throttle was advanced until we "were hanging on the prop", just above a stall. The up hill thirty-inch Tundra Tire touched the sloping hill and rudder was thrown-in to keep the airplane from "Ground-Looping", then the wide tail-wheel touched the sand, the throttle was chopped and I began "tap-dancing" on the brakes to stop the plane and avoid a "Ground Loop". The plane jerked to a stop, and then I came on with power to taxi to the top of the sloped bank to get above the high-tide mark on the gravel. We powered onto the flat area above the sloped bank, applied one brake and spun the airplane around to face the dark, silty water of Cook Inlet and pulled the Mixture Control, stopping all fuel flow to the engine. As the eighty-two inch Bore Prop came to a stop, I opened the right window and "latched it" to the underside of the wing and opened the lower door of the PA-18 Super Cub. I climbed out, and then helped Gary place his foot into the rear step and not onto the wing strut! After draining the coffee we had drunk on our flight over, we removed the fishing poles from the wing strut, I put on my Freighter Pack Frame with all necessary gear, except the container of cured salmon eggs. After slapping a few mosquitoes and gnats, we applied lotion to repel them and started walking toward the line of tall cotton-wood trees that lined the upper bank of the river's mouth.

We had noticed another Super Cub parked up on the flat area, and knew there would be at least one or two people fishing. As we made our way up the clear stream I saw that two young fellows were fishing in the "Sweet Spot", a hole that was favored by the large king salmon. I turned to Gary and quietly said that we would have to fish one of the other spots until they limited out, and left the river. This we did, and with no success.

As the sun was burning a hole in the western horizon, the other fishermen finally left the river and walked toward their Super Cub. Gary and I eased over to the "Sweet Spot Hole" and started flaying the water! "FISH ON"! I helped Gary land the king, and as we pulled the beautiful king salmon onto the gravel alongside the creek, I reached into my vest and from under my left arm I pulled a stainless steel Smith and Wesson Model 69 .44 Magnum pistol and gave the flopping fish a "Konk" on the head with the end of the six inch barrel, the fish straightened out and gave a little "Death Quiver" and lay still. I removed the hook for Gary and with my Buck folding knife, cut the gills to drain the blood from the fish.

Back to "Production Mode" we went! "Fish On" as I "set the hook" and brought a saltwater fresh king salmon flapping to the bank, I pulled my pistol and was about to thump it on the head, when a face stuck out of the alders and said, "How's it going?" I looked up and saw a man's head and at first I thought he was a "Fish Hawk", a game-warden checking licenses and limits. I said, "Not too bad. How is it with you?" "Not So Good!" he said. "I just put my Super Cub into the Inlet!"

I turned and shoved my fishing rod toward Gary and said, "Take this. I've got to go see if I can help him get the airplane out of the water!" Gary responded and grabbed my rod and fish. I followed the fellow to the Cook Inlet beach and looked out about thirty or forty yards or so to see the tail wheel of a Super Cub protruding from the water, the only thing showing of the airplane. When their airplane flipped onto its back and sank into the silt laden Cook Inlet, the two occupants had to open the door while under the cold, dark and dirty water, swim to the surface for air, and then to the beach. Fortunately for them, there happened to be a long rope tied to a large cottonwood log, high up on the bank, and had been used for beach set-net fishing. While dragging an end of the rope, the pilot had to swim out to the little plane as it floated on its back slightly beneath the water and attach the rope to the tail wheel protruding above the surface.

As we stood looking at the situation my mind was trying to analyze and come up with a solution to this problem! Gary soon joined us. The pilot of the submerged plane asked how we can get the plane out of the water. I told him to hang-on, I was thinking! About that time I came up with the idea. "Boys, grab the rope and pull as much slack from the plane as you can. With them pulling on the rope, I went and untied the knot near the log and pulled as much slack as I could get. I then tied a bowline into the line and went back mid-way in this loop, placed a three foot long stick into the loop and started turning and twisting the line. This formed a perfect, "Mexican Windless" and we winched the plane toward the shore. When I ran out of rope, I had them hold slack again, I un-wound the rope, untied the bowline and moved it outward toward the plane, tied another bowline and started winching again. This we did until we had the airplane within fifteen feet or so of the gravel beach. I knew the plane would be "high and dry" when the tide went out, as it was "flood" tide by the time we completed the winching operation.

After securing the plane, I asked the pilot what had happened. It seems the moisture in the air had condensate on the inside of the windshield of the plane and as he had nothing to wipe it off, decided to take-off with the windshield obscured, knowing it would soon clear as the engine heater-defroster warmed it. He should have left the right window open, stuck his head outside to see, and would have been able to observe what was going on. Instead, they lined up on the sloping beach and trying to squint threw the fogged windshield, pushed the throttle to the firewall, and began their run. As the plane gained speed, the plane drifted down-slope toward the water and when the right wheel touched the water, the plane turned about forty-five-degrees, and flew for a moment. Being the plane did not have enough airspeed, it stalled into the cold, silt laden dark water of the Cook Inlet. When the wheels touched the water, the plane flipped onto its back and sank! It was a miracle the passenger and pilot were able to get out of the airplane while under that silt laden water, and not drown. Many, many people have died in Cook Inlet with planes and boats, or when wading and their boots were captured by the soft, "quicksand" of many of its beaches.

When the tide receded, the plane was "high and dry" and the boys turned

it onto its wheels and drug it above
the high tide mark. Unfortunately they
did not salvage the plane for at least
five days, as I observed it sitting
there when I made a few more "fish
runs". I am sure the salt-water raised
"Billy-heck" with the electrical gear
and any exposed metal surfaces.

If they had recovered the airplane with
a helicopter and hauled it back to
Nikiski, they could have lowered the
plane into a fresh water lake to help
stop the salt effect.

"--IT Happens!" And It Did!

LATE FOR THE PARTY
(WIND-SHEAR ACCIDENT NEAR THE GLACIER)

It was the day for the party my wife was giving for her sister, who had just graduated from Beautician School. "Don't worry; I'll have him back in plenty of time for the party. We're only going rabbit hunting for a few hours", Chuck told my wife Sharon as we pulled away in Chuck's red Chevy pickup. I should have known better and stayed home! This was a direct invitation for "Murphy to intervene in our plans for the day!" The airstrip where his white and red Piper PA-18 Super Cub stood at the ready was only a few blocks away. As we approached the plane, the thirty inch tall Air streak Tundra Tires loomed into view, proudly holding the nose of the beautiful bush plane arrogantly into the air. A "Stud Horse Plane" if I do say so! The huge donut styled tires was designed to handle the soft tundra or sand, and also cobble and rocky areas too. This was a fine bird!

Chuck had called that morning saying his son had other things to do, and asked if I wanted to go rabbit hunting with him. I mentioned that I had installed my wheel skis on my plane, and wouldn't be able to land on the cobble moraine near the glacier where we usually hunted rabbits. "No problem!" Chuck replied. I just had my bi-annual (the proficiency check ride required every two years by the Federal Aviation Administration), and you can ride with me if you're not afraid too." I replied, "I'll sit in the back seat of your plane any time, as long as you are the one flying it!" (And still would!)

The flight would require a little more than an hour each way, but the weather was good with a few scattered clouds and an occasional light bump. When we descended from the high plateau to the lake area and slowed for the landing on to the cobble glacial drift between the glacier and the lake, we had a "sinker" or two on final. "Sinkers" are down-drafts, and are not real popular with Bush Pilots, and as far as that goes, most of the other pilots. Chuck skillfully added power at the right time and kept the descent constant until we thumped down; on the cantaloupe size cobbles of the gravel clearing. The landing gear made "chattering" sounds as we rolled over the rough area. I patted him on the shoulder to show my approval of the landing. He was a very skillful Bush Pilot and could get the plane into some very short strips. The thirty inch tall tundra tires absorbed the humps and bumps and easily traversed the uneven ground with small gullies. The plane looked like a "waddling duck" with outstretched wings as we taxied toward the thick alder covered glacial moraine ridge. Chuck skillfully braked and powered around an occasional boulder and when we reached the brushy hill, locked the left brake while coming on with power, and "blew" the airplane's tail around and parked with the nose pointing out from the brush in case the wind came up while we were hunting. "Good landing", I told him. He replied "Yeah! She was a bit squirrelly on final! A gusting wind is blowing, but not too bad!"

The bunnies were doing a good job of hiding. Chuck got a couple. I mostly stretched my legs. We noticed that the wind was very fickle, and had changed directions as we reached the steep rock wall that bordered the glacier on the north side. After cleaning the bunnies he had shot, we walked to the area that was to be used during take-off, tossed to the side any rocks that were too large for the cub to handle, and also cut one small clump of willow brush to give additional room for the take-off run. We would not be taking off toward the lake as was normal, but in a different direction. The wind was now blowing straight from the rocky mountain face about a half mile away. But there was plenty of room to climb and turn out toward the lake before reaching the rocky face, so Chuck chose to go into the wind.

I drained my bladder, as was usual before getting into the Super Cub; while Chuck drained the fuel sumps to be sure we had no water in the gasoline. They say an airport is the most "wet-on" piece of real estate around, and I believe them. Pilots and passengers alike "mark" the area before getting into the planes. I buckled up good and tight as Chuck climbed in and fastened his seat belt and shoulder harness. We both put our head-sets on, and after starting the engine and checking the magnetos, Chuck asked, "Are you ready?" I tapped his shoulder and said, "Yep. Let her go."

I could feel the strong pull of the eighty-two inch long Boer Prop as the engine wound up to full power! Within a few feet the tail wheel was off the ground and the only contact with Mother-earth was the soft tundra tires bounding and bouncing as they contacted the cobbles, transferring the shock through the landing gear, then I could see Chuck lean forward and quickly pulled the flap handle in concert with the control stick. The little plane actually leaped from the rough ground. We were now airborne and quickly were above the tall tree tops. Chuck, ever so gently, eased the nose of the airplane forward and cautiously bled from "full flap position" to the "no flap position", maintaining altitude as he did, sensing the

airspeed as if by natural ability. I
could feel the air speed increasing
rapidly. We were well above the trees
now, and "Doing good!" I thought to
myself. No sooner did the thoughts
pass the threshold of my mind, that a
second sense of something going wrong
loomed in my thoughts! The plane
started to feel very mushy, as if
"lumbering", very ungainly, and
overweight, not at all like it should
have felt. I was not at the controls
flying the airplane, but was so
familiar with Super Cubs that I
instantly knew something was wrong. I
looked at Chuck's left hand to see if
he had pulled the power lever back,
knowing that he had not. The throttle
was all the way forward and I could see
he had pressure on it. I looked at the
tachometer and the RPM was where it
should be, the engine was screaming,
but I could sense that we were starting
to lose airspeed. The wind had shifted
on us, and was now from our tail and we
were entering a "wind shear" situation!
About then, the left wing started to
fall or drop, and Chuck immediately
forced the control stick forward and
right, to keep the plane from stalling.
The nose dropped down and the wings
leveled, but we were going down.
Fortunately there was an opening in the
tall trees. "Hang on!" Chuck called
out. I already was "Hanging On!" The
tubing that formed the back of his seat

now held the permanent impression of my hand as I squeezed it so tightly! Bracing myself to keep from hitting my head or face on it as we crashed! The trees and the ground streaked toward us. Just before we hit the ground, Chuck pulled full flaps and pulled hard back on the control stick. "BLAM! SCREECH! GRIND!" We had hit hard on the large tundra tires which took most of the shock, but the "V" piece that held the landing gear together had snapped. Down the plane went onto its belly, spun around and slid a short distance and stopped in a cloud of dust. The engine was off, and both ends of the prop were bent and curled back and resembled a "Charles Atlas Advertisement!"

I patted Chuck on the back and said, "We'd better get out of here before she catches on fire!" Chuck flipped the master switch to the "Off Position", opened the door and crawled out with me in hot pursuit! "Are you okay?" I asked. "Yep, Praise the Lord for that," was his reply.

We both stepped away from the plane to observe the situation. We gave each other a hug of relief to see neither one with any bodily damage, only our pride at this point. We watched to be sure the plane was not going to catch on fire, extinguisher in hand. She was all fight. Chuck said, "Looks like you're going to be a little late for that dinner." "Yeah, but maybe they won't worry too much about us. They'll probably figure we had to wait for weather", I said. After a few minutes our pulse rates dropped down to the high end of the "danger zone". The blood vessels on my forehead were standing at attention, to say the least. I wiped the cold sweat with my bandanna, wrung it out, and wiped again.

After recanting the events, we were sure we had hit a "wind shear" or very strong "down-draft" and there was no climbing out of it. Wind shears have been known to take large jet airliners to the ground, and they have much more horsepower and climbing power. We were very fortunate to walk away from this one with no injuries. I was glad Chuck had enough wisdom and courage to point the nose downward and keep from stalling the airplane, and inevitability inverting into the "moose hunters stall". If you invert at a low altitude, they usually carry you away in a plastic bag, as the plane comes down vertically on the nose. We were too close to the ground for a recovery, if that had happened.

Chuck removed a small plastic water bottle from the plane and handed it to me and I chased away the "cotton balls" that had formed in my throat. He then did likewise.

We knew we would be here for a while, no getting out without help on this situation. Chuck gathered his survival gear and mountain tent from the plane and we looked for a good level, and soft spot to place the tent. With the small rocks brushed away, we spread a ground cloth and erected the tent. After this, we gathered a large pile of dry firewood because it would be difficult to find wood after dark. We each carried a small flashlight in our shirt pockets, along with a butane cigarette lighter.

At this point of my story, I'd like to inject an idea. If you do not carry a small flashlight now, think about taking up the habit! It could save your bacon! I always do. And I always carry a four inch crescent wrench and a small set of Channel-lock pliers in my pant pocket. Whether you choose to carry the tools or not, the flashlight should be a must. If the power goes out, or you drop something in the dark, or need to find the keyhole at the door, that light can be a lifesaver. Another thing, I am amazed to see how many men do not carry a small pocket-knife! If I don't have my "survival tools" with me, I feel as "Naked as a jaybird!" Carry the flashlight on your belt or on a lanyard around your neck, or somewhere within reach! A woman should carry a small flashlight in her purse or on a key chain. The small crescent wrench and pliers would be a plus also. There is nothing like being able to take care of the situation in time of trouble!

A tie down anchor, produced from under the rear seat, was screwed into the ground under each wing and a rope used to secure the wings, as we knew the wind would be blowing before the night was over. We were only a quarter mile away from the confluence of five glaciers which flow into a small lake. The winds can be fierce in this area!

As we still had sunlight, we started the job of cutting trees to build a large tripod, which with the aid of a cable hoist carried under the back seat of the plane, would be used to lift the aircraft. By removing the cowling and attaching the cable hoist to the engine "lift bracket", the plane would be hoisted high enough to check the landing gear and do any needed repairs. After felling and removing the limbs of one tree, we drug it next to the airplane. At this point in time, we were so exhausted that we decided to turn in. It had not been all physical exertion, but the stress of all the excitement. It had turned out to be a "bear of a day!"

The wind was merciless that night! We could feel the side of the tent being forced down and touching our face by the force of the wind, and it felt like the tent might be blown away, with us in it! That made for a long, restless night.

Up the next morning, we were shivering while getting the dry wood ready for the match. Chuck drained a little gasoline from a wing sump into an empty pop can, and poured this onto dry wood that was neatly piled within a circle of stones to contain the fire. Now a piece of paper was ignited with my cigarette lighter, and tossed onto the fuel dampened wood. "WOOOOOSSSSH" It was ablaze and before long we had a good "white-man fire". The old saying goes like this: "Whiteman build B-I-G FIRE, STAND WAY BACK!" "Indian builds little fire, "STANDS WAY CLOSE!" I think this fire would be judged a "WHITEMAN FIRE", even by the liberals, at least the first fifteen minutes of its life. We turned one side to the fire, and then turned the other side toward the fire, letting the heat penetrate the wool pants. With my hands on my knees, slightly crouched down, I warmed my rear pockets……sure felt good, and washed my hands by using snow from a drift found a few yards away. The cold, coarse grained snow melted as soon as it touched my warmed hands. Then holding my hands toward the fire, I rubbed them together until they were dry. Snow was scooped into a small pot from the emergency cook gear, and then placed on glowing hot coals that had been pulled from the blazing fire to the side of the stone circle. With a long green alder limb, that had been cut with a small forked limb still attached on one end forming a hook, I snagged the copper colored bail of the pot handle and pulled it from the coals, while using small pliers removed from the moose-hide leather pouch carried in my right pants pocket. This leather bag also contained a four inch long crescent wrench, toenail clippers, four inch Old Timer Muskrat Skinner pocket-knife, and a "Metal Match" (magnesium fire starter). The Metal Match is made of magnesium and flint and will spark even when wet.

There would be no coffee this morning, and man, do I love my coffee when I get up in the morning! Cocoa would have to suffice, as Chuck was not addicted to the caffeine as I am. Hot instant oatmeal was the main course with a handful of "Trail Mix" which consisted of a combination of nuts and raisins and other dried fruit. With breakfast out of the way, we surveyed the plane and went about the task of cutting two more trees for the tripod. After the trees were dragged close to the front of the plane, they were lashed together with nylon rope from the plane's survival gear. The tripod was then raised and positioned over the engine. With the engine cowling removed, we connected the small cable hoist that was carried under the rear seat of Chuck's airplane to the hoisting ring on top of the engine and to the nylon rope holding the tripod together. After ratcheting the lever enough to put a strain on the cable, we untied the ropes securing the wings to the anchor screws. The little hoist groaned as Chuck gave the last few strokes required to raise the airplane enough to crawl under it and inspect the undercarriage of the airplane. Writing on a small pad from my left front shirt pocket, we made a list of parts required to get the airplane flyable enough ferry it to Anchorage and be properly repaired.

Chuck thought Jimmy, a close friend of ours who had hunted this area with us before might be showing up at anytime……..but there was no sign of anyone or any other airplane that day. At one o'clock in the afternoon, it was decided I should hike a few miles to a cabin being used by trappers in the area. They had a small two-way radio in which a message might be relayed to friends in Anchorage.

I loaded "buckshot" into my Belgium made Browning Auto Five, three inch twelve gauge shotgun before slinging it over my shoulder. We had seen brown bear along the creek between us and the cabin, and I wanted some protection when going through the dense brush. If I spotted any "hasenpfeffers" I could replace the "double-00 buckshot" with number six shotgun shells.

The ground was frozen pretty firm in the clearings and the snow was not too deep in the woods, which made for easy travel. I tried to stay in the open areas as much as possible, passing up numerous bunnies that scurried ahead of me. I needed to get this message out as quickly as possible in order to get help on the way. After flushing a few mallards that were feeding in the creek, I reached the bank and saw hundreds of Sockeye salmon skeletons and carcasses with green head still attached, lying on the bottom of the shallow creek. Occasionally there would be one or two scarlet colored salmon swimming slowly around the pool, like disabled submarines listing to one side, soon to move no more. I hurriedly crossed the creek at a narrow spot, trying to step quickly enough to keep the water out of my boots. After an hour of steady walking, I came to the opening of a large swamp that bordered the lake. The walking was much easier along the firm sandy beach, and soon I was at the path that led to the cabin door.

The cabin gave the appearance of Edgar Allen Poe residing there for years. The dark water stained logs were shaded by the limbs of close growing birch and spruce and hemlock trees. Dark shadows covered the approach to the door. I walked up the soft spruce needle covered path to the door and knocked firmly, calling out, "Anyone home?" Just as I had expected, no sign of anyone! Today was the first day of lynx trapping season, and I knew the trappers would be out in the woods making sets, as I know I would have been! I opened the outer door and stepped into the enclosed porch area and stopped for a moment, to let my eyes adjust to the darkness. I could see the skulls of different animals that the trappers and hunters had taken over the years, hanging by nails and balanced on beams and rafters, most draped with spider webs, resembling a scene from "Indiana Jones and The Raiders of the Lost Ark". I knocked on the kitchen door, knowing I would get no answer, and then walked into the main room, which was much lighter with the sunshine penetrating through the large window facing the lake.

Stepping into the room, an old wood stove stood to my left. Along the same wall was a small table, cluttered with pots and pans and empty soup cans and such. At the far end of the room were two sets of bunk beds. Along the south wall which held the large window facing the lake and the path, was a larger table but also quite cluttered. I could see the breakfast plates still in place, along with maps, a flashlight, and cans of fruit and such.

The lid was not quite tight on the can of pipe tobacco that sat near the table's edge and the sweet aroma coming forth made me wish I had not given up the habit, reminding me of the time I almost always had a pipe in my mouth and one drying in my pocket, still warm from use. Sure looked tempting, but no! Better hold out! Just one pipe full of that good smelling tobacco would have put me on the hook again! To the right of the window was the battery used for the two-way radio. It was the idea of the radio and sending a message for help that had brought me here in the first place.

The room had the musky smell of fur animals. I could see signs of the earlier trapping as a few mink hides were still hanging while they were being dried, suspended from nails driven into the rafters and high on the wall above the door, still flesh side out. These hides would have to be turned fur side out before completely drying, as they might tear or crack during the turning process if they were too stiff. This indicated they had not been on the stretchers too long. The cabin had a good smell, reminding me of my earlier days on Bishop Creek. The stove had a hint of heat still remaining, and a skillet with long handled spatula rested on its top. After surveying the good supply of canned goods, I opened a can of peaches and quickly devoured them. I removed a one dollar bill from my wallet and placed it on top of the empty can, then proceeded to write a message to be left on the table in the place of the breakfast plates. I knew they would notice something had been moved and read the message, and hopefully be able to reach someone who could relay the message to our friends in town.

After waiting about two hours, and no one had showed up, I knew I'd have to be going in able to get back to the plane before dark. As I walked from the main room through the porch area, I noticed otter and coyote hides hanging from the rafters. With the door securely latched, I started the long walk back to the plane and Chuck.

For the return trip, I walked farther down the beach from where I had come and out of the woods, past the mouth of the creek before starting cross-country. Traveling this way, there would be less walking through the dense brush and the snow that had softened during the heat of the day.

For the longest time I could see the moraine in the distance, and it seemed to move out in front of me as I trudged along. Finally I came to the sparsely covered flat that stretched to the toe of the moraine where we had camped. Then, I saw Chuck walking out toward me, smiling. He told me about talking to pilot he had contacted with his airplane radio. The pilot would relay the message for us. I then explained what I had been able to do. We felt sure the word would get out.

The sun was about to set, and we did not dare leave the airplane suspended from the tripod. It would be too dangerous if the wind came up, and we knew it definitely would. We lowered the airplane and proceeded to tie it as snuggly as possible using the anchor screws we had retightened into the ground.

After eating, we fed the fire until late into the night, so as to be tired enough to go right to sleep. I didn't want to lie in the tent listening to the wind blowing and pushing the sides of the tent, with ropes snapping and popping when the gusts hit…and they would hit! Winds near this glacier can be fierce, as they can blow for miles with no obstruction before reaching this moraine area. The sky remained clear and the stars were out in force, but the moon was a sliver of fingernail, giving very little light. Well, time to hit the rack.

We were up early, standing by the crackling fire while searching the sky toward the lake and above the low mountain to the north, and listening intently for the sound or the "low humming sound of the Lycoming engines that powered the Super Cubs and the help they brought.

"I think I can hear an airplane," Chuck said. "All I can hear is the 'Egg Sucking Wind!" I replied! My ears were buzzing from the strain of trying to locate an airplane that wasn't there. I could remember the time when I'd been stranded by myself for many days on Whitefish Lake on the west side of Merrill Pass. The almost constant wind through the trees on top of the hills sounded almost like the low moan or hum of an engine. I had been stranded there for eleven days before actually hearing and seeing the Civil Air Patrol De Havilland Beaver that brought the needed gasoline. Well, that is another story!

"Yep! Your right, Chuck!" Two specks appeared below the slowly lowering clouds, far out over the lake. Behind us the clouds were settled against the snow covered mountain and the white face of the glacier, but out where we were past the gravel moraine, the clouds tapered upward, high enough to safely fly and the wind had died down by now. This was a good sign.

We ran out to the open area and motioned where to land, as they flew over us while looking the area over. On the ground, we guided them as they taxied toward the tripod and the airplane. The Super Cubs waddled like buzzards with their wings spread out to balance themselves, wing tips dipping almost to the ground as the huge soft tundra tires absorbed the cobbles and potholes.

After a few big hugs from dear friends, Jimmy came forward with a thermos of hot black coffee and a dozen or so "Pig in a Blanket" (pork-sausage-links wrapped in biscuit dough, baked and browned in his wife's oven at his home. Jimmy's wife, Dianne, had risen early enough to cook and carefully wrap the food in aluminum-foil so they would be fresh and warm for us! She knew, "That Vern will be starving, and I know he'll be having a coffee-fit!" She was right!

Back at the fire, we blessed the food and gave thanks for the safe trip the boys had made. Then, we dove into the grub! Oh, that coffee was so-so-good! The flavor of the sage and sausage spices had seeped into the biscuits and I thought I had died and gone to heaven when I bit into them! Now I am one person who enjoys good food.

In a short while, we were at the airplane and had it hoisted high enough again to work on the landing gear. We removed the damaged "V", the metal piece that holds the two landing gear shock struts to the gear legs and axle, and replaced it with a new one. One tab had to be "re-welded to the frame", and Jim had brought "oxygen and acetylene bottles and a welding torch" and did a great job welding it. With the experience of welding on the columbines and other farm equipment during his younger days, he was an artist with the torch and welding rod! When we went to install the new landing gear leg, we saw they had brought the wrong size gear-axle. Jim would have to repair the old gear leg or we would have to spend another day waiting to get a new one of the proper size gear-axle to be flown in from Anchorage. The weather was turning bad and we knew if we waited, it might be a week or two before we could get a flight back in with the needed parts. "I think we can repair the gear," was the reply of our mechanic friend.

Now it was time to replace the much damaged prop. Side-cutters were used to cut the stainless steel "safety wire" that secured the prop bolts, and then a 9/16" box-end wrench was used to remove the prop bolts. A few remarks were made stating the "damaged and curled-up ends of the prop" resembled a "Charles Atlas advertisement". The new prop was bolted on the prop flange and safety-wired in place. Then the prop was turned until the blade stood at the "six o'clock position", pointing straight down. A small willow branch was cut and "poked into the ground" just below the prop tip. This would give us a "reference point" to judge whether the prop flange or the crankshaft of the engine had been bent. The prop was slowly rotated to where the other end of the prop was in line with the willow stick, and it was the same distance and in alignment as was the other end of the prop had been. Now the crucial test, as the engine was started and we stood to the side of the engine and propeller and watched the prop as it spun around. There was "no variation" in its travel, which indicated the prop flange and the crankshaft were alright.

Chuck said, "Vern, you can ride with Jim. I don't want anyone in the airplane with me when I ferry it back to town." That suited me fine! Jim had a package of smoked salmon that we planned on opening once we were airborne.

The plane jerked from side to side as the wheels followed the contour of the ground. With a man steadying each wing, we slowly taxied each airplane over the cobbles to the take off area, and then we very carefully re-inspected the gear of Chuck's airplane. Everything seemed to be holding okay. "Looks alright", was the comment. Chuck eased the throttle forward and the one-hundred and sixty horse power Lycoming engine pulled the Piper Super Cub forward and then into the air! Off the airplane went, and with us in hot pursuit. I enjoyed eating smoked salmon and caribou jerky while flying back to town. I was sure thankful for the good friends who had come to help us in time of trouble.

Upon reaching our home airport, Chuck greased the airplane onto the gravel runway, a super smooth landing! After a short taxi, the airplane was secured in its "tie-down spot", like a good horse back to his stall after a long ride. Tomorrow the airplane would be checked over at a regular aircraft maintenance facility and a new landing gear installed.

A short drive later, we pulled up in front of my house. When we walked into the kitchen-dining area, Chuck was a bit "shy looking", which is not his normal demeanor. He told my wife Sharon, "Well, we're sorry we were a little late for the party." She explained that all the guests had been very worried, thinking we had "Crashed and were Injured" and could not complete our flight. Sharon knew about Bush Flying and had the feeling that we were alright. I said, "Praise the Lord, we made it again!"

A BIG "OH S--T!" AT THE O'MALLEY AIRSTRIP!

I don't recall the exact year, and I will refrain from looking it up in my "Daily Log" book. The names have been changed to "Protect the Guilty". If you are not a "Chechako", and have been around for a few years, this might bring back memories and answer a few questions.

I purchased my first Piper PA-18 Super Cub which was "tied-down" at O'Malley Airstrip in 1980, and I flew it for the first time on my birthday. My wife and three daughters and I lived about a block from the strip and it made it very handy, as my wife Sharon could see me flying in "on Final", and knew when to put the moose steaks on! I ran a trap-line that extended from Drift River to the south, and extended past Mount Susitna and up to Collinsville and near the Denali Park boundary. One winter, the wolves were in great numbers up near the headwaters of the Susitna River and taking the moose and caribou down faster than Tim and I thought they should be doing. Now Dang was a good friend and very good Bush Pilot, and we had done extensive flying together while searching for a missing "guide and his hunter". This was in a later year, and there was no construction work going on, so we decided to fly up north and

66

check out the wolf situation. The hides were bringing a good price from Louie Brunner and other fur buyers. The day was decided upon on which to depart, gear had carefully been selected, the firearms were zeroed-in and we had an ample supply of ammo, and the snowshoes were tied to the strut of the right wing next to the leather rifle scabbard that held my long range shooting rifle for fur bearers, a Remington Model 725 chambered in .244 Remington caliber. My up close and fast work rifle was a Ruger Ranch Rifle semi-automatic in .223 caliber with a Leupold 2x7 power scope attached and was inside the Super Cub to keep it restively warm, and easy to reach.

The morning we were to depart O'Malley Airstrip, the temperature was down near zero and a very annoying ground-fog had settled around the airstrip. We had loaded our Super Cubs with five-gallon metal gas cans full of gasoline to refuel the Super Cubs when needed, and I carried a galvanized "Tractor funnel" that was lined with a chamois cloth "filter or strainer" to keep any water or ice particles or debris from entering our wing mounted fuel tanks. My airplane's engine had been heated with a 12 Volt propane "Red Dragon" heater, while it was wrapped in an insulated engine cover to contain the heat. After it had warmed enough to allow the prop to be spun freely, the hot engine oil that had been heated on our cooking stove was added and the engine started and was allowed to run and heat up. After the engine temperature rose to the green section on the engine temp gauge, the engine was shut-off, and the insulated engine cover re-installed to keep the warmth in and allow an easy re-start after the fog dissipated. In the winter time, I always drained the hot engine oil into a metal two and a half gallon Eagle gas can, after the days flight. This way, I could re-heat the oil while in the can, on the burner of our cook stove at home before departing for the airport in the morning.

We waited and waited for what seemed like hours when Dang's older brother, Ding drove by to see how we were doing. He was talking about wolf hunting in years past, and when he got ready to leave, he interjected his opinion of the situation. "If you wolf hunters had any "Balls at all", you would get into your airplane and get going, and not let this ground-fog hold you back. It's only a thin layer hanging on the ground!" Well, Dang and I looked at each other, and decided to "get a higher perspective" from up the mountain side. We jumped into his pickup truck and drove up O'Malley Road and sure enough, the fog was a very thin layer, probably less than twenty feet deep. We talked it over, and thought if the stuff will "blow off the runway" enough to see for the take off, we will be able to climb above the fog in just a few seconds, once airborne.

Back at the airstrip, Dang said he was going to fire up his engine, taxi to the take-off point, and wait for an opening. I told him I was going to "top off my fuel tanks" as I had run the engine enough to allow a gallon or so to be pumped into the tank. I drove my Ford F-250 Crew cab truck with a one hundred and thirty gallon fuel tank with a 12 volt transfer pump, and began the job of adding the gasoline. Dang had taxied to the north end of the strip and the fog seemed to lift a bit. About that time, I heard his engine rev up, and I could hear the skis clattering on the hard-packed snow as he began his take-off run toward the south end of the airstrip.

Just at that moment Mother Nature in conjunction with the senior attorney named "Murphy", of the world famous "Murphy's Law Firm" decided to interject a little "foul play" into the equation. Just when Dang began his take off run, a thick cloud of fog blew in and grabbed the runway like an eagle catching a spawning salmon! Dang was "roaring down the runway" as the fog moved in, and seriously interfered with his vision. His right skis hit a deep groove or track in the frozen snow, which jerked him to the right, and the airplane turned almost ninety degrees to the runway, and ended up almost straight across the runway from where I was refueling my Super Cub! "BOOOOOOOM!" "CRUNCH!" A TREMENDOUS ROAR ERRUPTED!

I looked over to the other side of the runway in time to see a silver-colored spinning propeller and prop hub, flying high up into the air, making a beautiful arch similar to the "Great Land-mark in Saint Louis", and falling close to the now entangled Super Cub of Dang, and the Cessna 185 Bush Plane of his brother Ding! "Hot Dog!" this is an "Oh S--T of the Highest Degree!" The airplanes resemble a short legged pit-bull and a tall mastiff entangled in a "dog-fight!" Dang had run full bore into his brother's like new Cessna 185 airplane! The invoice for repairing the damage was probably past the one hundred thousand dollar mark and quickly climbing! I stopped my fueling operation and ran across the runway and helped Dang get out of his Super Cub, which luckily did not erupt in flames! As would be expected, he was devastated! "What to do now?" I walked back to my Super Cub and re-secured the tie-down ropes, as the "Flying was over for the day!" What an expensive "Wolf Hunt!" And we didn't even have any animals to skin!

An old friend of the family was notified of the accident, and he was to "break the news to Dang's brother, gently!" I think they chained Ding down before telling him what had happened, and only after he promised not to "kill his brother Dang", was he released!

Dang's Super Cub was towed back to its "tie down" location, and I went and re-tied the ropes securing my Super Cub. We had had enough excitement for the day! I didn't want to go wolf hunting by myself. I removed my Canadian made Three Star Woods sleeping bag, my camping supplies, rifles, and shotgun and drove home. The wolves were safe and could continue their carnage.

In the future, remember this little story. Don't get too cocky with your remarks! It could be your equipment involved! The wolf hunter had the "Balls to try and take-off, but not the Good Fortune to succeed!"

There is another way to look at the story, at least all of the damage was "kept in the family", and no "outsider" was involved! Murphy has a way of getting into the action! Keep your mouth shut and "Don't give him an invitation!"

POACHED EGGS AND MOOSE MEAT TOO

August 26, 1960, Tay Fish, an old friend of Doug's and a new friend of mine, and I were hunting moose down at my cabin on Bishop Creek. After spending the night at the cabin, we were up bright and early, had some breakfast and coffee, and stepped out of the cabin to do some moose-meat hunting. Now there is a difference between "Moose Hunting" and "Moose-meat Hunting". With "Moose Hunting", there might be an element of sport involved, but with "Moose-meat Hunting"; the sport element is set aside, and what-ever-it-takes to get meat for the table comes into play!

Tay was to remain in the vicinity of the cabin, while I walked and hunted up towards the large cleared fields nearer to Stan's homestead. We separated and I cautiously hunted my way toward the fields. After reaching the wide open area where Stan had planted his "Prove-Up" crop, I leaned against a tree and watched for any sign of movement of the bull which had been seen earlier in the fall, but there was none. After moving a couple of time to a more appealing location, I had finally decided there would be no moose activity in this location, this morning! Just starting to sling my rifle when a shot is heard, then another, and then silence, I thought,

"Oh my!   I hope it is a bull!", and started "hot-footing" back to the cabin!

After traveling about three-quarters of the way back, Tay appeared and was very much "Big Eyed". "Did you get him?" I asked. "Yes, I think so", was his reply. We finally slowed our pace enough to catch our breath when we reached the clearing below my cabin. "Where's the moose?"   He indicated that it was on the opposite side of the creek, straight across from the cabin, so we walked across the large spruce log bridge with heavy rough sawed timbers and then up the little hill and entered the woods, working our way through the sparse devils club and occasional alder thicket. Finally we reached the "Kill Site".

There lay a "Four Point" buck, as we call them. It was a "this year's moose calf" and the nubs had not reached the "Trophy Stage" as yet! Well, we were "Moose-meat Hunting" and this was moose-meat! The moose was gutted in short order, and across the creek we waded to the cabin for an axe to quarter the moose. There was no problem crossing the creek as we were in fashion for the season, and were wearing hip-boots. I tied the axe to my pack-board and we grabbed some extra rope, retained one rifle for protection and proceeded to the carcass. Tay held the legs apart as I used the axe to quarter the animal, and we each then tied a quarter of meat to our pack board. We each gave the other person a hand at getting the pack-board in place and the straps adjusted for the work ahead.

We both had to lean forward enough to retain our balance that we resembled Sherpa guides this a month's supply of food and gear on a "Mount Everest Attempt" as we trudged toward the cabin. When we reached the steep bank of the creek that was about ten to twelve feet above the water, we grabbed onto small birch trees to help support our weight as we backed down the hill, with Tay in the lead. As he neared the water, hung onto a thin birch tree that was not up to the task of supporting him! The tree started bending toward the creek and before Tay could regain his balance, made a tremendous "SPLASH" into the creek, ending up laying on his back and only his face protruding above the water! I busted out laughing, and was laughing so hard I almost wet my pants! I had to stop and take a leak before I could shed my pack and go rescue him! He was a-cussing at me to get him out of the water before he drowned! When we got to the cabin with the last load of meat, we both had a good laugh! Over the years, we pulled some pranks that only "the Mountain-Men" would do!

A friend, Jerry, had just completed work as a Stream-Guard monitoring the commercial fishing at Port Dick and was now working for Fish & Game in our area, checking licenses and hunters, and the game taken to be sure it was legal. We make no mention of shooting this moose, but he suspected something was going on. One day he made a surprise visit and appeared at the door as we were cooking some tenderloin steaks. We invited him in for coffee or cocoa, and before long he asked what we were cooking. I replied, "Just cooking up some scraps for the dog." As he got ready to go, he walked to the wood stove, raised the lid on the cast-iron skillet and peeked in. "It looks like Darn Good Scraps to me!" He walked to his state supplied truck and drove off, but later told me that he figured we had shot a moose, and maybe it wasn't quite legal. He said, "I'm glad no one ever said anything about it, or I'd have had to arrest you for it!" I could see his point. He had taken an oath and friends or not, had to abide by it!

WISDOM OF A RETIRED AND VERY "SEASONED" POLICE OFFICER

In the 1980's, when parked at a RV Camp in Seward, Alaska, my wife and I met a retired Criminal Investigator from the Atlanta, Georgia Police Department. He and his wife, along with their small dog, were touring Alaska and vacationing in their large "Land Yacht" RV. We became close enough friends that they trusted my wife to "baby-sit" their prized pooch while they enjoyed a boat tour around the bay.

I was drilling water wells in the Seward area, and we were parking in this campground as they had electricity and water and sewer hookups, which my wife very much appreciated. I was much more used to "Dry Camping" and didn't require all of the convenient things. In the evening when I would return to our RV after a day of drilling, we all sat around the camp fire and enjoyed each other's stories of the past. He sure had a "Doozy or Two", and I had a few of my own!

After one evening around the fire, the ladies were over talking by themselves, I told him, "I used to be a bit of a "Smart Mouth" in the past! I wonder why someone didn't try to Knock My Block Off!" The "Very Intelligent Police Officer" quickly interjected. "IT WAS THE PISTOL YOU WERE WEARING,

VERN!   IT   WAS   THE   PISTOL   YOU   WERE
WEARING!"   After   time   to   think   about
it,   I   believe   he   was   right!   "Walk
Softly and Carry a Big Hog Leg!"

THE FIRST ARCTIC CAT SNOWMACHINE ON THE KENAI PENINSULA!

Some people are held to the old ways as if their foot had been spiked to the floor! I guess I am one of them. The thought of getting rid of the dogs and dog sled was out of the question at that time! Besides, I seemed to be more gifted as far as working with animals and they almost always did their best for me. Besides, I had never done much "knuckle-busting" (mechanic work) with the wrenches on engines, and keeping an engine running was a mystery to me! Just how a magneto worked I just didn't comprehend. On the other hand, I didn't mind feeding and watering the dogs, mending leather harnesses, and trying to control them. A person did end up with a lot of "shovel work", but that came with the territory. The dogs were mighty handy when the thermometer's mercury dropped almost out of sight, I could bring the dogs into the cabin, have them hop up on the bed with me, and things got warm and cozy and stayed that way until morning, and when we all gathered around the cherry-red sided wood stove, and we would take turns scratching!

Comparing the Health-Hazard; I'd rather put up with the canine odors while mushing the dog team, than to be behind a gasoline powered machine, putting out those carbon-monoxide fumes! The petroleum laden fumes of the gasoline engines were terrible all of the time! I still remember walking behind an Evinrude Trackster, years later, as we made our way to a moose I had shot, and dang-near dying from the fumes of the "mixed-gas" (oil mixed with the gasoline). The fumes were so strong, I almost choked!

Now my trapping partner Jay was just the opposite. He had much more experience working on machinery as he had owned a Cushman Eagle Motorcycle; that kept his mechanic skills fine-turned! Jay could also see that the future belonged to the modern machines; the dogs were a thing of the past!

The original Arctic Cat side-by-side snowmobile was actually designed for professional foresters and the likes and not for recreational use; and was a heck of a work-horse, if you could keep it from vibrating itself apart! The traction with the machine compared to that of a light-weight dozer. Later in years I talked to Bert Johnson who owned B & J Surplus and was the first Arctic Cat dealer in Alaska. He informed me "I was almost ashamed to sell someone the machine without also selling them a welder to keep it together!" Back then, there were no "self-locking nuts", or Lock-tite "Thread Lock", and the bolts would vibrate loose.

I was in Anchorage for some reason or another when Jay first showed me the brand-new red colored Arctic Cat snow-machine he had just purchased! This was the machine where you sat side-by-side, and had an engine mounted on the drive frame behind you. The throttle and brake levers were located in the center section and forward edge of the seat, and the shift lever was behind the driver next to the four cycle Kohler engine. A round steering wheel resembling a metal horse-drawn cart wheel with spokes was located behind the large Plexiglas windshield that usually was fogged or very dirty, so we stood much of the time while operating the machine. The Arctic Cat had oak track slides mounted on the under-side of the frame assembly that was connected together with steel channel-iron drive cleats. Between the steel cleats nylon belting the width of the track was attached for flotation in the deep snow. The thing felt and acted just like a small dozer with very poor steering as you "clank, clank, clanked" your way down the trail. Jay told me to take the thing up to the upper Hillside area of Anchorage and give the Arctic Cat a good test run, handed me the keys to his little pick-up and he went back to work. Well, Doug was with me and we drove the pick-up as far up the hillside of the mountain as we could, then I backed the truck against

80

a snow covered bank next to the road. There we parked the truck, started the powerful Kohler engine, shifted into reverse and throttled up to engage the centrifugal clutch, and we were able to back the machine off the truck with no problems. Sitting side-by side on this marvelous thing, with the engine oil warmed to operating temp, I threw the whip to it and we proceeded to climb up the side of the snow covered slope like a home-sick mountain-goat. It was almost scary the way that old Arctic Cat would climb, with the wide steel cleats! Finally we got up so high; I was felt like I was getting "light headed" and thought I might be starving for oxygen! I told Doug to hang-on to the uphill side of the machine as I tried to turn the thing around, on the steep slope. Another benefit: this machine was much wider than the present snowmobiles, and it would not tip-over very easily. With the thing now pointing downhill, I released the brake and we took off like a High-speed Toboggan at the final run of an Olympic Competition! I'm glad the thing didn't have a "recording speedometer" because I probably would have had a heart-attack when I saw how fast we were traveling!

We had no time to get scared! We were hanging on with everything we had, and no time or opportunity to scrutinize the situation! I pulled the throttle back to slow the machine; instead of slowing, we sped up as the centrifugal-clutch disengaged and we jumped into "Oklahoma-Over-Drive!" I applied everything we had as far as the breaks were concerned, and that wasn't enough! We were traveling so fast that when we reached the bottom of the valley, with all of the momentum motivating us, we kept going about a third of the way up the opposite hill! It is no telling how many clumps of scrawny hemlocks we had massacred that day! These machines were never designed to be fast, but I think Doug and I had un-knowingly set the worlds speed record for the Arctic Cat 500!

One occasion while spending the night at Earl Daniels cabin, the following morning when Jay checked the oil dip-stick there was sludge built-up in the dip-stick hole. It appeared that the oil level was up in the operation range. It was "Colder than a Montana Well-diggers Hinny" when we stepped aboard the trusty machine. Jay pushed the throttle lever ahead, and the clutch engaged and off we went "clank, clank, and clanking" across the snow covered lake. It was not long until the "clank, clank" sound of the track was over powered by the sound of the "clunk, clunk, clunking" sound of the engine, as we had run out of lubricating oil! The engine seized-up! Now the "Head-Scratching!" What to do now! The engine was removed, placed on a small sled, and skidded back to Earl's cabin and disassembled and the crankshaft smoothed with crocus-cloth, and reassembled with fresh bearings. That was a good lesson! Better to have this happen close to Earl's cabin than to happen miles away in the bush! When I think as to why I tend to favor dogs and horses, I can remember no time when a dog "seized-up" because he hadn't been fed! That says something for the animals!

We were having success trapping and were thawing and skinning beaver in my Bishop Creek cabin, and were greasy and sweaty and smelly, needing a bath or shower, or at least a soaking in Clorox water to "freshen-up". Well it was minus twenty degrees outside and with no galvanized wash tub large enough to get in, so there was no chance of a bath happening at the cabin! There was a water hole cut in the creek-ice where we dipped the bucket and retrieve the tea-colored tannin stained water and climbed the steep hill to the cabin on Bishop Creek. We thought, "Hey, it's Sauna Night at the Tauriainen house tonight!" At their homestead we were always welcomed by Art and Mimi and their Finnish family to use their log sauna building to clean-up. It was probably in "Self-defense"! Jay and I decided to hop on the Arctic Cat and drive down

Bishop Creek to Leo's house and then over to the Tauriainen house. We always enjoyed the fellowship there.

I was wearing "Double-Pants"; I had a pair of light-weight wool pants inserted into a pair of heavy corduroy pants and was sewn together at the cuff of the legs and at the waist and had suspender buttons installed for keeping the "rigging up"! We were wearing military surplus canvas mukluk boots with the heavy full-length, knee-high felt insert. Jay went outside and coaxed the Kohler engine to life. I made sure the barrel stove had plenty of green birch, enough to keep the fire going long into the night. As everything was in the "Go-Position", I turned the wick down and blew out the flame in the kerosene Aladdin Lamp. It was now "Blacker than the inside of Dicks Hat" in the cabin! I fumbled my way to the door; helped slightly by the moonlight filtering through the tall spruce trees that were standing alongside of the little log cabin, and penetrated the four foot wide window openings covered with translucent plastic sheeting, a cheap substitute for window-glass.

As we started down the trail, we soon reached the narrow section of the creek, where the hills on either side of the creek almost came together, and the bottom was choked with alder bushes, forming a thicket! We had chopped a narrow trail through this area and a person had to go slow to keep from getting the wide front skis of the machine tangled in the alder. Once we passed the alder thicket and narrow section, the scenery broadened, opening up into a wide, flat swamp. Due to the extremely cold temperature, the snow was very "Squeaky" as we made our way past the confluence where Daniels Creek entered Bishop Creek. A few hundred yards farther, the hills on both side of the creek pulled away from each other, as if they had been insulted and wanted no more to do with each other, leaving space for the growing bitterness of the swamp with its dwarf-like black spruce trees to move in and form a huge wedge between them. This swamp opened to a huge and almost panoramic area of flat snow-covered muskeg and scattered with spindly black spruce trees here and there, as if pimples on a chocolate-eating teenager's fore-head. It was still early in the winter and the creek was "Making Ice" and was "talking to us" as the sounds of the expanding and splitting ice could occasionally be heard as it "Boomed" and expanded, sending a long crack down the ice of the creek. As we neared the confluence with the creek draining Timber Lost Lake, a cloud drifted into position to cover our view of the moon, as if someone placed a large umbrella below the huge butter-yellow colored yard light, shielding the soft moonlight's glow on the snow covered frozen creek. I had a flashlight which I carried inside of my military surplus parka to keep the batteries warm and shucking my Arctic mitten, I reached my bare hand inside and removed the light. We were traveling on the left side of the frozen creek, just a few yards from the bank. I told Jay to watch for open water and get over toward the swamp. We had just passed the beaver dam that formed a pond section where I usually had good luck trapping mink and otter, and I had once caught a beautiful wolverine there. That wolverine is another story!

We now had open-water on our right side that was caused by the heat from the swamp-gas just below the confluence of Timber Lost Lake. Instead of moving to the left and away from the creek, we remained straight and about that time I heard the "BOOM" as the ice gave-way! The Arctic Cat gently rolled to the right as if doing a "barrel roll of an acrobatic airplane", and promptly sank into the dark tannin-colored water of Bishop Creek, depositing me in the open water. Immediately my temper soared and soon a dark blue-black haze of fog hung over the open water as I vented my assessment of the situation! I began to turn the cold arctic night air a hot indigo blue with my exclamations! I treaded water as I threw the seat cushion to Jay who stood on the firm ice. He was given ample time to get off the machine and onto the firm ice as the machine did a slow "wing-over" away from him as it slid off the breaking ice and into the dark and frigid water. I'm afraid I lost my temper as I rang-out with a few, (maybe more than a few) obscenities. I swam to the edge of the ice and Jay helped me crawl up and onto the ice.

I knew I was in trouble with these water soaked clothes on. If they froze on me, it would be like wearing a culvert pipe casket around my midsection and metal stove-pipe for leggings, and Jay would have to drag me to the cabin like a frozen seal carcass! As soon as I was able to stand, I began doing "Deep-Knee-Bends"! If you could have seen me, you would have thought I was making a TV advertisement about the virtues of calisthenics! Within a minute or so, my pants were frozen as hard as steel pipes! The only place that would offer movement was at my knees and thighs as the "Deep Knee Bends" kept that section from freezing solid. This movement crushed the ice as it formed, and allowed movement of my legs. There was nothing we could do now except try to get back to the cabin as quickly as possible before hyperthermia set in! I looked like the "Tin-Man" from "The

Wizard of Oz" as I shuffled my way to the cabin. There was no danger of frosting my ears, as they were red with the rage seeping out! Well "--it Happens", and it did!

Once into the dark but warm cabin and the Aladdin Lamp was lit, I stood for a long time beside the wood stove as it radiated its life saving heat, a large puddle of water formed at my feet as the ice thawed, and I was finally able to get the stiff clothing removed. Oh Boy, the "Warm Sauna Thought" had fermented into a sad evening as we racked our brains trying to figure out how to salvage the snowmobile!

By the next morning my soaked clothing had dried as they hung from a sixteen-penny galvanized nail driven into the top log of the cabin's back wall. I had been able to put on fresh long-johns, the only positive thing resulting from my cold bath in the creek. I dressed and after breakfast we walked down the creek, surveyed the situation and walked onward along the creek to Leo's cabin, and told him what had happened. We then all walked over to Art and Mimi's house and while having coffee and home-made bread freshly toasted and buttered, tried to come up with a "War-Plan". The kids had received a round metal, saucer shaped sled for Christmas and Art thought it might be enough to keep the track form dragging on the ice as we pulled the machine down to Leo's house, "IF WE COULD GET THE MACHINE OUT OF THE CREEK!"

We took with us Art's block-and-tackle, axe, extra rope, long pry-bar, and a thermos of hot coffee as we walked toward the sunken machine. When we arrived at the location, we cut skinny spruce poles and hooked the windshield of the machine, and pulled it to the surface. By laying poles at an angle, we were able to form a sloped ramp upwards from the snowmobile and onto the ice. It was a slow procedure getting the Arctic Cat out of that predicament, but finally it was on top of the good ice! The drain plug was removed and we drained the water diluted oil into a can to be later burned. With the rear track section lifted and placed onto the metal "saucer" sled and the wide steel skis offering little resistance on the glassy ice surface, we easily pulled the machine to Leo's cabin where the engine was removed and placed into the basement to dry alongside the wood fired barrel stove. After a few days in the warmth, the magneto had dried sufficiently to produce a "spark" and the engine was re-installed onto the "lifeless red machine", fresh oil added to the crankcase, and with clutch-belt in place. The seat cushion was dry and ready for use, so we fired the engine, and "clunk, clunked" our way back to the cabin! Without the generous help of our friends, the red Arctic Cat snowmobile would still be shown on the charts as a "Navigational Hazard" in Bishop Creek!

LOCAL NEWSPAPER ARTICLE:
"VETERAN WOODSMAN TREED BY MOOSE!"

The harsh, cold winter had lost its grip on the land and the leaves were budding and blooming and a shade of green blanketed the woodland bordering the sparsely gravel-covered trail from my cabin. Earlier, the trail was so slick and muddy it was hard to stay upright and not slip and fall on your fanny! The sun had returned from its winter vacation and was again working at warming the surroundings. With the wind's help in removing the moisture from the exposed soil and surrounding woodland, the trail was drying, and was allowing for much easier travel. Jay, my trapping partner and I had walked from the cabin on Bishop Creek out to the Halbouty Road, and out the three miles to the mailbox located the junction of the North Kenai Road and the Halbouty Road. I was expecting one more check from the "Maas and Steffen Company, the Standard Fur House" that was located in St. Louis, MO, where I had mailed the brown burlap bag containing the last beaver pelts of the season.

We were returning from the mailbox, not too enthused with our results of "No Check" in the mail! My dog Compadre was walking about thirty yards ahead of us and minding his own business. Jay and I walked side by

side as he lead his dog Tok, a large
Malamute male that was used for the
"wheel dog" (dog closest to the sled in
the dog team). Tok could not be
trusted to run un-leashed, due to the
fact that he was so stubborn and "Bull
Headed" and refused to obey commands
and would quickly run off chasing
anything he could find to chase! Many
times he had chased and caught
porcupines and ended up looking like
his face and head was a "Pin Cushion",
and had to be chained to a tree until
he fought to exhaustion, before we
could start pulling the painful quills
with their "barbed" ends.

As stated, Compadre was leisurely
walking toward the cabin, when all of a
sudden a "Mad Mamma Moose", with ears
laid back and Hackle extended, charged
out of the brush on the left side of
the graveled Halbouty Road. As a dog
normally does in a situation like this,
Compadre started running back to his
Master, which was me! "Hold on, Jay!
I'll shoot my .44 Magnum in the air to
scare her off!" The rawhide loop over
the pistol's hammer was quickly flipped
out of the way, and as the pistol was
being raised above my head, I
automatically cocked the hammer of the
"single-action" pistol! "BOOM" The
revolver "ROARED" and our ear drums
started "Ringing" and the moose never
lost a stride! She was bearing down on
us like an Alaska Railroad locomotive

92

roaring down the mountain into Seward! "Run for the trees!" I hollered at Jay, and we made a dash for the woods! We reached a large spruce tree just in time to hide behind it and separate us from the cow moose. She chased us at least three full turns around that tree! All the while I had my loaded and cocked pistol barrel about one foot from her head! I didn't want to shoot her as I knew she must have just given birth and was trying to protect the calf.

Finally, Compadre charge in to protect his Master, and was nipping at her heals. She turned and started chasing Compadre, who looked like a golden-brown flash as he sped away! Jay took the short chain which was attached to his Malamute Tok's collar, quickly snapped it around a nearby spruce tree and climbed like a "Seasoned Coon Hunter" to the closest limb. "Get up to a Higher Limb! I'm coming up too!" I hollered to him! He quickly made way for me and before the moose could return her attention to us, I was up and sitting on a comfortable limb!

The "Mad Momma Moose" returned to our tree and stared at us, then took her vengeance out on Tok and started chasing him around the tree which he was tied to! The chain was almost "smoking" on the bark as she chased the Malamute! I told Jay that I would shoot her if she caught the dog. I was not going to let her kill or maul our dogs! Compadre charged in again, and after unsuccessfully chasing Compadre, she finally had vented her rage enough to return to the woods where lay her calf.

Needless to say, we rolled and smoked and enjoyed a few Bull Durham cigarettes while sitting in the tree, giving The "Mad Momma Moose" time to calm down or move her new offspring to a more secluded location! I reloaded my .44 Magnum before climbing down from the tree, and we crept quietly past the last known location of the cow and calf moose, and then "Shifted In to High-Gear" as we "Sprinted" toward the safety of the cabin!

The story was retold to a few friends, and years later while visiting an old friend Leo who lived much farther down Bishop Creek from my log cabin, he asked if I had seen the article in the newspaper telling when I was "treed by the moose". "No" I replied, and he went to an old desk, opened the drawer and produced a copy of the Newspaper with the article that had been written by Donnis Thompson, a regular contributor to the paper, who along with her husband Stan, owned the property where I had built my log cabin when I first came to Alaska, as I had been too young to obtain a home site or homestead land from the state. The spelling of my last name was incorrect, but the rest of the story was factual! "THE VETREAN WOODSMAN HAD BEEN TREED BY THE MOOSE!"

TRAPPING MY FIRST WOLVERINE

The trapping season was three days old, and I had placed many traps in likely places for the mink and otter that frequented my area. A few days before the season opened, I had mushed my dog-sled along my trap-line while checking for tracks. At a pond formed by the creek being slowed and held back by a beaver dam, I had spotted the tracks of a nice wolverine! These were the first wolverine tracks in this area in many years, I was told later. The beaver trapping season would open later.

I had accumulated over one hundred traps of various brands ranging in quality from "Blake-and-Lamb" all the way up to the prestigious "Oneida and New House Brand". The temperature was about ten above and ideal for making sets, so I looked the pond area over for a place to "way-lay" that wolverine if he were to return this way. Along the barren bank stood a black spruce about five inches in diameter at the base, and within two feet of the water's edge. I noticed a depression on the water side of the tree and chose this for my ambush site. Using my Hudson Bay axe to "shovel" the snow from the depression, I placed the head section of a salmon in the depression, lay a nice bed of dry straw from a clump along the creek's bank, I then replaced my gloves with a fresh pair and placed the "cocked-and-ready" Oneida-New-House 114 Jump Trap with teeth! I secured the chain with six wraps of Trapper's Wire around the tree and cut a shallow grove in the snow in which to hide the chain. With the trap set and ready, I located a slab of frozen "crust snow", trimmed it to fit the hole and gently placed it to show no signs of danger! I must admit, I was proud of the set I had made, and had high-hopes for it.

A couple of days had gone by since setting traps on the down-stream side of my trap-line. The snow was crisp and crunchy as the dogs and I sledded down the creek to check the traps. When we passed the confluence of Daniels Creek and reached the ninety-degree bend, the dogs perked their ears up and were sniffing the air. I thought there might be a moose in the area and kept my eyeballs-peeled! After making the sharp turn we were headed to the little pond area that held my wolverine set (in actuality, this set was good for land otter, coyote, lynx and mink), the dogs noticed something circling the tree. At first I thought I had caught a porcupine in the trap and was disgusted just thinking about it!

The closer we came to the tree set, the faster the dogs ran! We were blazing along the frozen ice that was lubricated by the one to two inches of snow cover. I finally saw the animal was moving too fast to be a porcupine, and realized it had to be a wolverine! As we neared the circling, snarling critter, I could see the dogs had vengeance on their mind and showed no signs of slowing as I tried to stop the sled and hollered "Whoa!" Finally as a last resort, I tipped the sled onto its side and hung on for dear life! They finally stopped about twenty feet from the snarling wolverine who kept circling the tree where he had excavated about six inches of the frozen ground trying to escape. His adrenalin was up, and mine was climbing!

I removed the Marlin Model 80DL rifle from the sled, worked the bolt action, placing a .22 short hollow-point bullet into the chamber and eased close to the tree that held him. I sighted threw the peep sight and along the barrel towards him as he made a couple of more turns around the tree, then he stopped and stood still and glared at me, snarling as I squeezed the trigger, the bullet entering his head between his eyes and just slightly above and ended his misery. He retained his beauty, even in death. The area was heavy with the wolverine's scent, which slightly resembles the smell of a skunk, but not as offensive to me. I removed the cruel trap from his forefoot and took the animal to the sled and let the dogs inspect it. They sniffed the carcass and slowly backed-away, showing a slight sign of fear. It took me about fifteen minutes to re-make the set. With the warm wolverine in the canvass bag that was strapped in the sled, we mushed on, down the frozen creek we sailed, with spirits high! Not many trappers are smart enough, or lucky enough to catch the Wiley Wolverine! But I had joined that fraternity of "the Elite"!

Many trappers have lost hundreds of dollars in valuable furs to a wolverine when it discovers their trap-line and travels up and down the line, eating the valuable fur animals that are in the traps, before the trapper can retrieve the furs! Many years later, I had a very large male wolverine eat my trapped martin on my trap-line on the south-east slope of Little Mount Susitna Mountain, when I was flying my ski equipped Super Cub to work my trap line. This beautiful large wolverine was such a prized catch, I had him life-sized mounted and he stands guard on the front-room log wall of our home on Daniels Lake now! I'll tell you that story later!

Down the creek we sailed across the snow lubricated clear ice until I reached Leo's cabin. I was greeted warmly as usual, and he was very surprised to see what I had caught, as he didn't think there were any wolverines in the area, as no one had seen any tracks. He had just read a story in the Field and Stream Magazine about a wolverine that tore a hole in the roof of a trapper's cabin and attacked the trapper! It was almost like introducing Leo to a Serial Killer! Leo said, "Let's go to Art and Mini's and show them the wolverine", and so we did. After a few cups of hot coffee and slices of fresh baked bread, I re-harnessed the dogs and made my way a few miles farther to Earl and Florence Daniels' cabin located on Daniels Lake.

When I began my trapping career, I relied on Earl Daniels to show me the proper way to skin and stretch the fur animals. I had messed up when skinning my first land otter by not skinning it close enough to the hide and left too much fat and flesh to be later removed! Earl said that was a "No, No!" Skin the animal as close as you can on the first pass, and you will not have the hard work of "fleshing the hide" and take a chance of cutting a hole in the hide. It is much easier on the first pass! Earl and Florence had once trapped and operated a mink farm at the mouth of the Little Susitna River. After Elmendorf Air Force Base was put into operation, they had problems with the mink "not breeding" due to the roaring sounds of the large military aircraft as they dropped low and slow in preparation for landing. The mink were not accustomed to the loud noise, and I think it might have given the female mink a "headache"! Earl and Florence moved their operation to Boulder Point which is further down Cook Inlet and north of Kenai and is near the East Foreland. While commercial fishing in the summer and running a trap line and fur farm in the winter, Earl discovered the lake that now bears their name.

Earl was all smiles when I showed them the beautiful wolverine and I relished the praise he bestowed on me for being clever-enough to catch the animal. When it came time to skin the animal he drove two nails into a honey-colored log not far from the Ashley Air-tight Wood Stove for me to suspend the animal on while I skinned it. Poor Florence highly protested the idea saying "He might cut the musk-gland and stink-up-the-house!" But as it usually is, the man of the house had the last word, and I was given permission to skin the wolverine in the warm house, as Earl reminded her of the below-zero temperature being too cold to properly skin the animal outside.

Before hanging the wolverine, I carefully removed the fur and hide from the lower back-legs and feet, and then using nylon parachute cord, hung the wolverine by the back legs so I could gently pull and carefully cut and remove the beautiful hide. I had removed the hide from both legs down as far as I could go without cutting around the "bung-hole". I resembled a surgeon performing a major operation in a life-threatening-situation as I gently carved the hide and as I neared the gonads I cut a fraction of an inch too deep and hit the "Musk-Gland" and the odor immediately permeated the room! It was like having a gang of drunken skunks in the living room flatulently "breaking-wind"!

And as many women are prone to remind their husbands when he has made the wrong decision, Florence belted-out "I told you so! I Told You, Don't Let Him Skin that Thing in the House!" It was too late; it was all over but the crying! No need to remove the wolverine from the nails and go outside now! Our eyes began to water! The odor would linger for days before completely dissipating. If ever you entered a room where a wolverine had "let off a little perfume", you know what I'm talking about! It was about like taking a full blast of "Mustard Gas" in the nostrils!

The year is now 2010 and the two nails used for skinning the wolverine are still embedded into that spruce log and are a reminder to me of when "I skinned the wolverine in Earl in Florence Daniels cabin!"

SLEEPING IN THE TREE TOPS
WITH BROWN BEARS BELOW

A couple of young friends from our church asked me if I would fly them out to a good location for silver fishing. They stated they could not afford the rates of an air-taxi, but would gladly trade "sweat equity" in the form of labor for the trip. I needed a short rock wall constructed and informed them if they could build the small wall for me, I would take them to one of "my favorite fishing holes". Within a short time, the boys gathered a load of rocks from the Turnagain Arm area and the wall was soon completed!

I flew a Piper Su[per Cub and could only carry one passenger comfortably at a time, so decided to fly Jason, who was the elder of the two, down that evening, catch a quick limit of fresh slivers for myself and return to Anchorage for the night. The following morning, I would fly Jeff, who was not yet eighteen years of age for a day of fishing. I did not want to take a chance of leaving the younger boy by himself in this area, as there were many brown bears that also fished for the silver salmon in this good location, and didn't want the responsibility of explaining to his parents, as to how their son was killed and eaten while "in my care". The older of the two was in his twenties and had hunting experience so I figured he should be able to take care of himself. After all, I had come to Alaska when I was only eighteen years old, not knowing anyone in the state, built a log cabin and lived where there were many bears in the area.

The days were long and warm and it had been a beautiful July in Alaska! My red and white Piper Super Cub 4302 Zulu was a joy to fly, and we were talking back and forth on the "Intercom Mode" where our conversation was held within the aircraft, and not broadcast over the radio waves for all to hear. The airplane was so finely rigged, I could place my coffee cup on the dash in front of me and take my hands off the controls and she would fly straight. In a no crosswind situation, if I wanted to make a turn, all I had to do was lean hard against the side in which I wished to turn, and she gently responded in that direction! With the strong 150 horsepower engine and the long 82 inch Boar Prop, I could get in and out of very short strips. Many strips were short enough, I had very little competition from others trying to land and fish or hunt in the same area!

The Kustatan River was loaded with fresh run, metal bright silver salmon swimming upstream to spawn. One fishing hole was farther up river from the Cook Inlet, a very narrow opening and very rough sandy strip in the alders with a few very tall and lonely cottonwood trees standing as sentinels near the upstream threshold to keep the less experienced "Bush Pilot" from trying to land. To land in this area a pilot needed the tall, soft and very flexible "Tundra Tires" to absorb the shock and bumps that awaited him. This fishing spot was comprised of narrow openings in the alder, and were suited to the lone fisherman.

Where I chose to drop Jason and his friend was toward the lower Kustatan, and consisted of a very long and wide sand strip that lay diagonally to the river where almost any airplane could land as far as length of airstrip. The requirement needed was tires wide enough to support the weight of the plane in the soft sand. From this long and sandy strip ran a narrow "dozer trail" through the alders and to the extremely silt laden river. Not used as a landing strip by most, a few of my friends and I who tried to stay "very practiced up in short-field landings" sometimes landed along this narrow "dozer trail strip" to avoid a long walk carrying fishing poles, container of fresh cured salmon eggs and an ice-cooler. If we were to make the long walk, we usually strapped our gear to an "Alaskan Freighter" pack-board and carried it on our backs, to leave one hand free for firearm use if needed! To be on the safe side, I had chosen the long strip and we parked the Super Cub at the end closest to the river. I did not want to taxi down the rough "cat trail strip" and park that close to the river, due to the heavy brown bear traffic. The bears sometime become interested in what might be in the airplane and rip open the fabric to have a "look-see".

At the river, we turned and walked along the narrow trail up to an open sand bar area that offered room for at least five or more fishermen to work the water at the same time. Also in this area was a submerged sandbar that protruded at least twenty five feet or more into the river and offered a nice "hole or pool" on the down current side. Many times the salmon swam up the current and congregated or "rested" in this "hole or pool". I had "ambushed them" many times at this location in the past, and planned to use the same strategy this evening!

Hip boots were in fashion, and were my attire, and were rolled down to the knees for cooler walking. Now at the fishing location, I unrolled the rubber tops and secured the belt strap to keep them from sagging down. My spinning rod was assembled, and a firm clump of cured salmon eggs "speared" onto the shiny, sharp single hook, and the translucent blue monofilament leader forming an egg-loop" was used to

106

help hold the egg cluster on the hook. I had been shown this procedure by my good friend and "Master Fisherman" Chuck Gold, and I had tied a fresh batch of these leaders just a day or so before!

At times I tend to be just "a few notches above Lazy" and had devised a rod holder to insert into the water's edge and support my fishing rod while relaxing or resting or doing some other chore, while still keeping my bait in the "sweet spot' and not have a fish grab the bait and run and drag my rod into the river, never to be seen again! This had happened before to me when a silver salmon hit the line and ran off with the rod and reel, before I invented this device!

Jason was carrying across his back on a black nylon sling a short barreled Mossberg 12 Gauge shotgun with Buck-shot and heavy Rifled-Slugs for protection against any possible bear attack! I, as always was wearing a Lawrence Quick-Draw shoulder holster with a stainless steel six inch barreled Smith and Wesson 44 Remington Magnum, and with my finger imprints filed into the custom fitted walnut grips, this revolver acted as "an Extension of my Arm" it fitted so well.

The time was getting away, and the burnt-orange sun was just a notch above the western tree-line, two metallic bright silver salmon were captured on my nylon fish stringer and tied to my rod holder at my feet as I stood in the silt laden water waiting for another "strike' to complete my daily limit so I could fly back home. Jason was up from me about ten yards, and fishing the main channel off the tip of the sandbar, when a movement caught my eye. I turned toward the brush covered bank and saw two large brown bears resembling "sumo wrestlers" or "professional football players" walking toward me, noses twitching and turning as they sniffed their way toward my string of fish. "Jason, we have company", I said, and he immediately un-slung his Mossberg and stood at "Port-Arms". "I'll shoot next to them into the sand and scare them off," I said and pulled the pistol from the leather holster, and sighted about two feet to the left of the leader's foot. "BOOM" the pistol recoiled, the sand flew into the bear's face, they both casually stood on their hind feet and each turned a circle as they looked around! They then dropped onto their front paws and started the slow walk towards the "larder" on the nylon stringer!

Get ready Jason! I'm going to scare them off or get them on us!" I shouldered my Smith and Wesson and began running toward the bears while slapping my hands together and hollering as loud as possible in the "meanest tone of voice I could muster". "ARRRRRRRRRRRRRRRRRRRRRRRRRRRRRGGGGH!"

The two surprised bears stood up, quickly looked at me, dropped down on all fours and spun around and made a dash for the safety of the alder patch! All we could see was their furry fannies as they vanished into the dense thicket. We both sighed with relief! I didn't want to shoot and kill the bears, but I had no place to go! Someone had to leave! It was either them or us!

I finally landed my last silver, quickly removed the gills and gutted the three fish, placed them into a plastic bag and inserted it into my Alaska Freighter pack-frame bag and we looked the situation over. It was now dark, "Blacker than the inside of Dick's hat!" The bears were moving into the river to feed and we could hear them downstream of us, trashing in the water, and growling at each other. We had noticed an old square metal five gallon can that had once held the job description of "Chevron Pearl Oil" (kerosene) container, and had floated downstream from a cabin far up river where a commercial fisherman and hunting guide had once resided. With my fishing rod dissembled and secured to my "Alaska Freighter" pack, I picked up the discarded fuel can and gave it a new life! It now became my "Little Drummer Boy" percussion instrument as I started beating on the can as we walked toward the "dozer trail" and on up to the waiting Super Cub. Jason had thought of camping near the river, but after being advised to camp at the large upper strip away from the bear traffic, he quickly took my suggestion!

Fortunately I had a very good landing light installed on my landing gear that lit up the runway in front of me. After many, many night landing at the un-lighted O'Malley Airstrip with no problems, the night land would be no problem, and I bid Jason "Adieu!" As I roared off in the semi-dark sky, Jason quickly erected his pop tent, rolled out his sleeping bag and crawled in. But having no "Nocturnal Knock-Out Pills", "Restful Sleep" was not to come! I found out later he lay on his back with the 12 Gauge Mossberg cradled across his chest, intently listening for sounds outside. His vigilance was soon rewarded by the sound of two bears walking closely around his tent, and sniffing for treats that might be inside the tent! Jason thought he might soon become their midnight meal! He decided this situation must change before they had a chance to "Open the Package"!

Making as much noise as possible, he climbed out of his sleeping bag, put on his boots and coat and with his Mossberg slung across his back, climbed the nearest birch tree large enough to offer a "Roosting Area" for the night! And long and painfully uncomfortable was his perch on the narrow limb!

"Good Fortune" came early as Jason was "Paroled from his Tree Limb Prison" when my good friend and early riser Chuck Gold landed for an early morning harvest of the metal bright silver salmon with his "Master Fisherman" buddy Ray. Upon landing, Chuck taxied his 93 Charlie Super Cub down the narrow "cat trail strip" to a little clearing that offered a parking near the river.

Back at the ranch, I had scorched two chunks of caribou Polish sausage and two eggs, encased them in toasted slices of that nutritious "Wonder Bread White", wrapped them in plastic wrap and would eat them during the flight to the Kustatan River. I met Jeff at the airstrip about six o'clock, the plane was refueled, windshield cleaned of the numerous green bugs that had been deposited the flight before, and we were soon on our way. When we reached the Kustatan River and slowly flew over our little fishing spot on the sand bar, "Dipped my wings" as I spotted Chuck and Ray with fishing lines in the water, and laying on the dry and warm sandbar stretched out on a blue tarp was a very tired and weary Jason, in deep sleep! At first glance his six foot plus body was sprawled out and looked as if he had been shot and killed, but not yet gutted!

With the Super Cub now safely landed and parked, Jeff and I walked to the river with fishing rods in hand. I waved at Chuck and he walked over and asked "What kind of friends do you have?" I asked him "What do you mean?"

Chuck said he had landed his Super Cub and was taxiing down the "cat trail strip" towards the river when he noticed a fellow running behind him with a short barreled shot-gun at the ready! When he stopped the plane and opened the door, Jason came running up within a few feet and was very surprised the pilot was not me! "What can I do for you?" Chuck asked! Jason said he thought the plane belonged to his friend Vern! Chuck asked, "Do you always go chasing your friends with a loaded shotgun in your hands?" We both had a good laugh!

When I walked over to Jason as he lay sleeping on the sandbar and called out his name, he opened his eyes and started telling me about having to climb the tree to get away from the brown bears, as he was too scared to sleep in the tent! We had a good time while quickly harvesting our limits of silver salmon, loaded the plane with the bounty and I started flying the boys back to town. After two round trips, they were safely delivered to their waiting vehicle at O'Malley

Airstrip. I had to use a very "Stern Tone of Voice" to get Jeff to be the first passenger back home, as he wanted to stay and fish longer while I flew Jason back first. "No Deal!" I was not going to leave the young boy by himself with all of the brown bears in the area! I had to tell him, "NOW BOY, YOU GET INTO THAT AIRPLANE BEFORE I HAVE GET ROUGH WITH YOU!" And although he begrudged being the first person out, he decided he didn't want to see what means of force I had in mind! I still have never gotten used to children "Telling me what to do!"

Well, the boys had their fish, and I had my little rock wall! No one had been "scratched up or chewed on", but my friend Jason will never forget!

"SLEEPING IN THE TREE TOPS WITH BROWN BEARS BELOW!"

KNOW WHERE THAT BULLET IS GOING!

It was around 1963, and I had hitch-hiked into Anchorage to visit with my friend Doug and his family. The following day after I arrived, I received a phone call from Ron, a friend who worked in the meat department at the Safeway grocery store located on Gambell Street. He and his wife with two small children had moved up from Arizona in their customized Willys Jeep Wagon with a Chevy V-8 engine installed. I had met him through mutual friends, Mom and Pop Caffery that had lived on Halbouty Road while proving up on their Trade and Manufacturing Site on Daniels Lake.

I had hunted earlier with Ron on a spring black bear hunt, when we drove up into the Palmer Creek area, located near the Resurrection Trail and the small town of Hope, Alaska. I remember traveling up the steep, winding road, with the Willys Jeep Wagon-Chevy conversion moaning and groaning and creaking and squeaking and showing the muscle of the 283 Chevy engine! That thing would go! We waded through snow up to our thighs while going after the critters! We had experienced a good time hunting together and talked of going out again.

When Ron learned I was in town, he called and said friends of his had just come back from a successful caribou hunt near Paxson and the Denali Highway. He would be leaving early the next morning and driving up for a quick hunt and wanted to know if I would like to come along. It took me about as long as a hungry hound dog to down a fresh baked and buttered biscuit, and answered, "Yes, I'll be ready in the morning." I didn't have my snowshoes with me, but Ron said he had an extra pair to bring along, and he had an army sled in case we needed it. We would bring along his Army surplus pack board and my Trapper Nelson Pack-board. Don't worry about the food, his wife would pack sandwiches, moose polish sausage, and the likes! Heck, I was getting hungry just thinking about it! They really knew how to put on a feed!

I was looking forward to hunting with Ron again, and was in the process of getting my gear together. I had even brought my Custom .30-06 Springfield rifle into town, and as always, I had my Ruger Blackhawk .44 Magnum revolver, with the ammo belt full of bullets. If I had not had the rifle, I could still have made the hunt with the pistol, as I have shot many big game animals with the .44 Magnum pistol. My mukluks were propped up near the heat to dry the moisture from the one-half inch thick, full length felt liners, with canvass outer shell.

I was thinking about hitting the sack, when the phone rang, and it was

Ron wanting to speak to me. It seemed that a friend of his from work wanted to go caribou hunting with us in the morning. I don't believe Ron had ever hunted with him before, and it was for darn sure, I had never hunted with him before! I listened to Ron telling what a good chap his friend was, and then I finally interjected, "Ron, you know how particular I am about the folks I hunt with. I really don't know this feller, so I think I'll hold off on this hunt, and maybe we can go together again on a later hunt. He sounded a little "let down" about me backing out, but said maybe we could get together when he got back from the hunt. He would fill me in on the hunt and all of the fun I had missed. It sounded good. "We'll get together when you get back!"

I don't really remember what I did the next day, probably spent some time at the sporting goods store or at the B & J Army Surplus store on Northern Lights Boulevard talking to the salesman, Red, where they sold some of the first Arctic Cat snow-machines in Alaska. These were the ones that you sat side by side, and the engine and transmission was in back of you, almost like a small dozer. They were real work horses, but they seemed to vibrate themselves apart! Dang near needed an arc-welder with you at all times to keep them together.

Later that evening I remember that fateful phone call from Ron's house where Mom and Pop Caffery were babysitting. There had been a tragic accident. One of the hunters had accidently been shot!

As the story goes, the boys had driven up the Glenn Highway to Glennallen, had coffee and gassed the Willys Jeep conversion, and started up the Richardson Highway. All went well as they passed Gakona Junction and Hogan Hill, and a few miles before Paxson, they started spotting caribou amongst the spindly, stunted black spruce trees. Finally, they spotted caribou fairly close to the highway, stopped the vehicle and got out to take a shot at one. The caribou was wounded, they thought, so decided to go in after it. With the long Alaska Trail Snowshoes strapped to their warm boots, they reached the area where the caribou had been standing when they had first shot, and picked up the tracks (spotted the tracks in the snow and began following them). After following along to where the animal went into the trees, they decided to separate to cover more ground. Ron went to one side of the tree, while his hunting partner went to the other side of the tree. They worked their way along, now separated from each other's sight.

As they made their way along, and after thirty yards or so, Ron's hunting partner thought he spotted something on the other side of the tree where he was now standing. He stared threw the brush and was sure he could see the movement of a caribou on the other side of the clump of trees, so he raised his rifle, sighted carefully and squeezed the trigger. "BOOM", the high powered rifle barked! The animal immediately went down, so the hunter reloaded and carefully walked around to the other side of the trees, and stood as if overcome by a blast of a frigid arctic wind that stripped all of the warmth from his body. There to his horror, lay the body of his hunting companion, Ron, who had been shot in the head, and now lay dead in the cold snow! And all of the "If only I had it to do over again", and the "If I could go back in time!", and all of the "Oh S--t!" will never bring him back! A terrible, history changing mistake had been made, and no way to correct it!

I would hate to have that scene filed in my memory bank! I must admit, I cussed and hollered, and stomped, and cried! And when I finally came to my senses, said a little prayer for Ron's family that had to go on with life, her without a husband, and the young children without a father!

I have thanked my Father many times, even though he was not present and could not hear me, for hammering the safety aspect of shooting and hunting into my brain. Never take a shot unless you can see the animal well enough to "call your shot". Not just hit the animal, but be able to say exactly where the bullet will hit the animal. Do not "Flock Shoot" into a herd of animals (shoot at a group of animals instead of at an individual animal), and No "Sound Shots" (shooting toward a sound in the brush). If you can't see the animal well enough to see exactly where you are aiming, DO NOT SHOOT! Always be aware of where the muzzle is pointing, and never point it at anyone or anything you do not intend to shoot, and never treat a firearm as though it were un-loaded. CONSIDER ALL FIREARMS AS IF THEY WERE LOADED! AT ALL TIMES! NEVER USE THE SCOPE OF YOUR RIFLE TO OBSERVE ANYONE! These are just a few things to keep in mind. And I hope your hunting and shooting is a safe one.

THE NEAR "DODGE CITY SHOOT-OUT" AT SOURDOUGH CREEK!

Designed by Bill Ruger of Ruger Arms, the Original Ruger Black Hawk .44 Magnum pistol of mine has been used to put small and large game on the table or stop whatever was needed to be stopped, in defense of life or property. I have always tried to be on the right side of the law, didn't like fighting that much, and didn't do any bulling of any kind. My Dad always taught us to use gun safety and never point a firearm at anyone or anything that we did not intend to shoot. I always tried to heed his advice. About the closest I ever came to having a "Dodge City, Wyatt Earp type shoot-out", was with this pistol. I was once challenged to a shootout by a cocky dude that was much older than me. I later learned he was a Detective for the Alaska Railroad. I was twenty three years old at the time, tough as leather, and not an ounce of fat on me. I could carry out a moose quarter that weighted more than I weighed on a pack-board. The railroad detective had threatened to shoot my dog, Compadre and then challenged me. I responded by handing the leash that held my dog to my hunting and trapping partner, Jay. I squared off with the Railroad Detective and pushed my handmade fringed leather moose hide coat back, exposing the walnut grip of the Ruger Blackhawk .44 Magnum. I tied the quick draw holster to my leg and unhooked the rawhide hammer loop that kept the pistol from unintentionally coming out of the holster, and told him, "Any time you are ready!" "Time Stood Still"

It was the fall of 1963, Jay my good friend and trapping partner and I, with my Golden Lab-German Shepherd mixed male dog, Compadre, had walked from our camp along a seismograph trail that extended west of the Richardson Highway, just a few miles north of Sourdough, Alaska. After gathering supplies in Anchorage, we had driven up for a winter's meat supply hunt. As it was too late to find a camping spot when we arrived, the first night was spent at Petty John's Sourdough Lodge where for five or ten dollars per night we rented a semi-clean bunk bed to sleep in and an all you can eat breakfast. It was home-cooking and I didn't complain about the spot or two of coffee and gravy on the tablecloth! After a huge stack of pancakes covered with so much syrup you would have thought we were "placer mining", we headed north to a seismograph trail to locate a good camping spot.

As we were stretching the tent on the ground in-preparation of setting it up, a young fellow came over and introduced himself as a Fish and Game employee and wanted to check our hunting license. As Jay and I were "Pranksters" at times, Jay told him we did not have a license as we were "meat hunting" and not "sport-hunting". Oh my, the poor guy started sweating and I could see he did not want to try and arrest us, so he told Jay we should go and buy a license before we started shooting any game! Jay reintegrated, "We don't need a hunting license, we are not hunting for sport, we're only hunting for the meat!" After a few minutes of that, I finally said, oh, he's just joking and we produced our license for him to see. I could see the relief on his face!

Our camp consisted of my old Army surplus wall tent supported by smooth spruce poles whose limbs had been burned off during a previous forest fire on the Kenai Peninsula. As you opened the canvas flap, about three feet inside and on the left side stood an air-tight wood stove, light weight gun-metal blue steel with a stove pipe protruding through a gray galvanized metal chimney stovepipe adapter installed in a hole that had been cut in the thick canvas roof of the tent with a hunting knife. An Ovaltine-brown colored tarp replaced the exotic wool carpet that a noble might have required. When stoked and fired with the dead and dry, scrawny black swamp spruce firewood that was plentiful in this area, the "woof-woof-woofing" sounds protruded from the oxygen starved light metal stove, sides of which soon turned a cherry red and in turn radiated the BTU's making all inside the tent, toasty warm, and drowsy at times. As the tarp heated, it emitted a paraffin fragrance that filled the eight foot by nine foot room. Two military surplus cotton-tick mattresses and military surplus down sleeping bags were piled along the side of the tent. Far enough from the stove to keep from overheating, a wooden Standard Oil Blazo box and a wooden Standard Oil "Pearl Oil" box held Bisquick for pancakes and pan bread, corn syrup, slab bacon, canned corn and green beans, salt and pepper, coffee, box of tea bags, a large bag of raisins, a block of binder (cheese), a box of Pilot Bread, and cans of sliced pears and golden peaches. But always in a place of honor, if we were eating high on the hog, was the heavenly tasting Darigold Sweet Cream Butter, sealed in the one pound round can, and used only for special occasions. Ole-Margarine, which we nicknamed "salve", retailed at one dollar for five pounds, and was used for regular cooking, and the difference in quality was easily detected. When we opened a new can of Darigold Sweet Cream Butter, Jay and I always surveyed the beautiful yellow contents and drew a line down the center to divide the highly prized, rich tasting natural butter. One side was for Jay, the other was for me. "Woe" to the feller who took butter from his partner's side of the can! THAT WAS A "NO-NO".

The Darigold Sweet Cream Butter was too expensive for us to use all of the time, and was purchased as a special treat, used on special occasions like celebrating the receipt of a check from Maas & Steffen Company, the Standard Fur House in St. Louis, Missouri, for the mink and otter pelts that had been mailed to them. Or to be used after the first caribou or moose was downed, and the liver and onions were cooked along with fried potatoes and the store bought bread warmed in the thin steel skillet and spread with the heavenly Sweet Cream Butter! If you have never had an opportunity to go hungry from the lack of grub in the cupboard, or hungry and little food in your pack, or no dry spot to stop and cook a bite to eat along the trail, and still have to walk for miles with your stomach growling like a caged tiger, you can't appreciate what it was to "chow-down" on such fine vittles.

When light was needed in the tent, a Coleman gas lantern hissed while hanging from a hook formed at the end of a short piece of black trapper's wire that had been wrapped around the ridge pole and twisted to lock it in place. The wire is sometimes called "bailing wire", but as we had no hay to bail and our main use for it was trapping, hence our name. The brilliant glow of the silk mantel radiated light threw the clean and clear glass globe, and generated additional heat in the canvas walled room, releasing a slight petroleum smell to be blended with the other odors that were awakened by the warmth that filled the room; a hint of fried bacon grease, the musty smell of drying boots and socks that were suspended from a parachute cord wrapped around the smooth spruce pole that formed the ridge support of the tent, sweat scented long sleeved turtle-neck under shirt tossed onto the sleeping bag, along with a pair of long-john bottoms with knees and waist band stretched past original dimensions and a hint of "skid marks" at the seat, and the ever present, reassuring evergreen smell of spruce sap and wood smoke. For a quick light-source, we had a four foot long stick inserted into the Blazo box, standing vertical like a post, and on top of it was an empty can whose top had been removed with a P-38 army issue can-opener. This was slid over the erect stick, candle wax melted onto the now flat surface of the can's bottom, and the base of the candle quickly placed into the melted wax until it cooled and formed a solid base for a candle, as if brazed in place. If one

had to get up during the night for any
reason, such as to drain the bladder,
the candle could be lit, and not have
to mess with pumping the Coleman
lantern. The Coleman lantern would be
used for a major light-source such as
cooking breakfast. During the Alaskan
winters, it is always dark when you get
up, unless the "bed-bugs had bitten
you" and you slept until 10:30am! That
was not my style.

About ten feet from the wall tent
stood a freshly erected tri-pod made of
black spruce poles, the limbs and twigs
had been removed with a razor sharp
Hudson Bay axe. Cross beams were made
of additional black spruce poles and
were lashed horizontal onto the legs of
the tri-pod. This simple structure
would support the quarters of caribou
meat, after the shooting was over and
the gutting and skinning had taken
place, and the life sustaining meat had
been brought in from the field to be
hung. The caribou skins would be
spread out to dry and be used for
sleeping mats or robes with the hollow
hair insulating our beds from the
frozen ground. We also brought the
caribou fore-legs into camp to skin and
give to an Indian family we had met
that was also hunting in the area.
These forelegs would be used for the
upper part of the mukluk boots they
would make. The soles would be made of
ugruk (bearded seal) skin, as they were

from the old school. Now-a- days almost all of the mukluk bottoms are made of cow or horse leather. The ugruk skin is much tougher than regular leather soles.

With a few left-over pancakes spread with strawberry jam and rolled like a burrito and wrapped in a brown paper bag, Jay and I, along with my Golden-Lab-German Shepherd dog Compadre had walked on the seismograph trail to a low hill, narrow and long, and resembling a whale's back. We climbed the hill, slipping and sliding occasionally, my L.L. Bean Maine Hunting Shoes throwing snow. These boots were light as a feather and water-proof as long as the water did not come over the fourteen inch elk-tanned tops. I wore two pair of Wigwam wool socks in the un-insulated boots, which were comfortable in the winter as long as I kept moving. My mukluks were hanging in the wall tent and would be used when a lot of standing around was anticipated, or the mercury dropped out of sight! The colder it is the cruncher and squeaky the snow is when walking!

Jay, Compadre and I had spotted a band of caribou headed our way as we glassed from the hilltop. They may have smelled or scented our camp, or possibly us, and they turned and headed off to the right of us, not getting within good shooting distance. It was too early in the hunt to start shooting at them from a long range and taking a chance of wounding and having to track them and making for a longer pack. We eased our way down the hillside to the snow covered swamp with a few blades of dead grass sticking up, and made our way toward the trail that lead back to camp. When we were about sixty-five yards from the trail, we spotted a fellow walking on the trail towards us. Compadre was about twenty-five yards ahead of us and spotted the man and began to bark. I immediately called, "Compadre, heel!" As always, his response was immediate and he turned toward me and made a bee-line to my left side, where he remained, hackle still up, but tail wagging. Compadre's loyalty to me was one hundred percent! The stranger walked to within forty yards of us and it was at that point in time that the man broadcasted, "I'm glad you called your dog when you did or I would have shot him! I'm tired of having someone's dog trying to bite me when I'm in the woods." I asked, "You would have shot him?" He replied, "Yes", and he looked straight at me in a threatening way and threw a challenge to me by saying, "And if you want to go?" I took this as an invitation to a "Dodge City type Shoot-Out". I had never had an invitation like this before, and normally would have passed it up, but he had threatened to shoot my dog!   Now that is a different matter!

I calmly reached down and put a leash on Compadre, and handed the leash to Jay as he stood at my right, and then moved farther away to the side to be clear of any stray bullets, and started grinning like an "opossum in a persimmon tree." I opened my handmade moose hide leather coat with fringe along the bottom to help drain the water during a rain, and hooked the soft leather coat behind the stag handle of the custom Ruana skinning knife that was looped on the brown leather belt holding my wool trousers in place. I secured the rawhide-leather holster tie-down thong to my right leg, to keep the holster from gripping the pistol barrel and slowing it as it would be drawn upward to clear the holster and turned forward to line up on the target. I then eased the leather hammer loop that kept the pistol from bouncing out or being knocked out of the holster while walking in the brush or while running, or riding a horse, or working. With the moose hide coat pulled back exposing the faithful Ruger Blackhawk .44 Magnum I was ready for action, and looked the gentleman in the eye and said, "Anytime you are ready!"

I learned a few years later this man worked for the Alaska Railroad as a Detective, was packing on his belt an eight inch plus barreled Smith and Wesson .22 Remington Jet in a very protective type leather holster with flap to cover the pistol grip. This new model comprised of a .357 Magnum brass necked-down to .22 calibers and was slung on his belt in a cross-draw fashion. I was packing a Ruger Blackhawk .44 Magnum with six and one half inch barrel in a western style "quick-draw" holster and I had no doubt that I could "clear leather" before he could. After running hundreds of rounds of custom hand-loaded ammunition through this gun, I regularly neck and head shot spruce grouse and ptarmigan with it. After a long pause, he cleared his throat and spoke up to warn me of his prowess with his pistol, stating he had shot rabbits out to thirty five yards. I then told him of putting three out of five 250 grain Keith designed hard cast bullets into the chest cavity of a wounded caribou while it was quartering from me at a measured three hundred and thirty three paces. Time Stood Still. And so did his gun hand! Finally, the railroad detective's hackle started to settle back down. After clearing his throat a couple of times, he confessed that my dog Compadre had not been a real threat to him. Jay and I knew all the time Compadre had not been a threat! As all of this took place, Jay stood to the side holding Compadre' leash, grinning

from ear to ear and rubbing his hands
together, and just waiting for the
action to start! Jay had seen me make
too many good shots with that pistol
for me to miss a target of that size as
close as we were.

The Alaska Railroad Detective had over
stepped his grounds.

SMOKEY, THE ALAKSAN MALAMUTE CHAMPION

When we moved to the lower Hillside of Anchorage, our property was large enough for a big garden spot, which produced in abundance, a huge front lawn for enjoyment, and a horse lot in back. I have always loved horses, and still do, so we purchased a Shetland-horse mix mare named Gidget, and what a "Fire Ball"! After breakfast and the girls were off to school, I usually went for a ride on the trails not far from our house. Sometimes, Sharon and I rode double on Gidget, as she was as strong as an ox, very sure-footed, and had black hooves almost as hard as flint and never required shoeing! When we started our ride on Gidget, our Malamute dog Smokey would jump and howl and raise so much cane that I thought I'd better take him with me just to keep him quiet, and also to keep him from breaking the chain!

I still had a couple of dog-sled harnesses that I had used back in the early sixty's when I lived and trapped on Bishop Creek, on the Kenai Peninsula. I had purchased the harnesses from Earl Norris and his wife, the owners of the "Howling Dog Farm" which was located where the University Center is now along the old Seward Highway. I ended my short time at the newly built Alaska Methodist

132

University to go trapping. The college degree would probably have made life a little easier, that's for sure!

The dog collar I was using was from Canada, and was in the style of a leather horse collar, and was stuffed with hair to cushion against the breast area. A dog could comfortably pull a much heavier load with this type of rigging as opposed to the racing type harness. Each day after I got Gidget saddled and ready for the ride, I put the work harness on Smokey, the heavy harness leather straps came along his sides and were attached to a hardwood "single tree" as used on a plow-horse set-up. A four or five foot rope lead from the single tree and was attached to an automobile tire that was mounted on a steel wheel. It didn't make any difference whether the tire was aired up or flat, as it was drug laying flat on the ground, plowing the snow in front of it. This put a real drag on things, especially when we got a fresh snow. This drag was little concern for Smokey, as he followed along behind me as I rode Gidget along the trails.

Christmas came and gone, and it was February, 1974, and the Anchorage Fur Rendezvous was coming up soon. One of the events that interested me was the "Dog Weight Pull Contest", where dogs were divided up and placed in their weight category to see who could pull the heaviest sled. Now I had never done anything like this, so when Alaska Mill and Feed put on a demonstration pull, I went down to check it out. Seeing how the pull was run, I practiced a few days with Smokey pulling a heavy sled and me in front of him, giving him the signal to start and pull the heavy sled about twenty-five feet across the finish line.

The morning of the Fur Rendezvous Weight Pull contest finally arrived and we were getting ready to enter Smokey in his first official competition. As we were starting to leave the house, one of our three daughters said, "Let's pray that Smokey wins the weight pull!" I replied that it would not be fair to the other dogs to pray that way, what we should pray is; Smokey will do his best." We were in agreement, and prayed likewise.

When I placed Smokey on the scales to see in which category he would compete, his weight was seventy-nine and one half pounds, placing him at the bottom of seventy pounds to one hundred and twenty pound, or Middle Class. Before long, the contest started with the Light Weight Class up to seventy pounds pulling first. After this was over, Smokey's Middle Weight Class started. As I had never done this before, I entered Smokey in each round, starting with the lightest pull and every pull there-after. The pros in this event, held their dogs out of the contest until the weight was up to a few hundred pounds, so as not to tire the dog out on the earlier pulls. The pros hadn't paid much attention to Smokey and me until we got up to about a thousand pounds, and then they drifted over to where I would be standing, and asked, "Just who are you, where are you from, and what's your dog's name?"

Smokey proved to be about the most disciplined dog out there. When it came time for us to make a pull, he sat beside the sled while I made the hook-up to his harness, and remained quiet until I got in front of him and gave the signal to start the pull. With this signal, I called, "SMOKEY COME!" I got to my knees and slapped the frozen ground. If the sled's runners had frozen to the ice, he stepped to the side, and lunged forward; causing the sled to twist and turn enough to break the runners loose, then he strained and tugged until he was moving fast across the finish line! THE CROWD LOVED IT! They would roar!

Slowly, the other dogs and trainers dropped out of the contest, as their dogs could not or would not pull the heavily loaded sled. Finally all the competitors had dropped out and we were at two thousand, three hundred pounds. Just to prove Smokey was the champion, I told them, "Put another one hundred pounds on the sled!" When I gave the command for Smokey to start his pull, he stepped to the side, gave a tremendous lunge, and the sled started creaking on the frigid ice, and he made the pull with the crowd roaring and cheering him on. I still do not know the maximum weight he might have pulled if I had kept going!

No, it would not have been fair to pray for Smokey to win the contest, but it was fair to pray for Smokey to do his best! The last pull was a total of two thousand, four hundred pounds, and I think he probably could have pulled more, but we had won fair and square, and there was nothing more to prove.

After the pull at the Anchorage Fur Rendezvous, I entered Smokey in the weight pull in Wasilla, where he won his weight class and came in second place in the Heavy Weight Class, with some dog in that class that weighed over one hundred and thirty pounds!

I then took Smokey to Soldotna to enter him in the weight pull down there. He again won his class and came in second again in the Heavy Weight Class! Many years later, I was visiting a family in North Kenai, and met one of our competitors in the seventy to one hundred and twenty-five pound class held in Soldotna years before. I remembered the competition and this fellow had entered a very large husky-type breed that weighed about one hundred and ten pounds. From the appearance of the dog and handler, I guessed them to be our real threat, if we had one. As Smokey and I waited for the competition to begin, this was the only dog that gave me concern! As it turned out, the dog did not do very well, whether the crowd spooked him or not, I don't know, but I was glad to see that he was having an "Off Day" and did not pull! The fellow's wife was still very upset that they had lost the competition, but that's the way it goes sometimes.

A Side Note: After winning the Anchorage Fur Rondy Weight Pull, I received a phone call from the owner of a huge Saint Bernard that scored very high in the Heavy Class. The gentleman wanted to come out to our house for a "VISIT?" He was very friendly and as we sat drinking hot tea and munching on moose summer sausage and smoked king salmon, he asked me how I had trained Smokey, and spoke highly of his very "disciplined nature" and pulling ability. I thought nothing of sharing with him, until later. Not long after visiting and gleaning the information on my training method, he published a book on the subject "Weight Pull Training For Your Dog" The book contained much of the information I had so freely given my recent guest!

"NEVER LEAVE A CHECHAKO WITH A FUELED-UP CHAINSAW UNLESS HE IS PICKETED!"

My wife Sharon and I live on the beautiful Daniels Lake, north of Kenai Alaska. A few years after we moved into Earl and Florence's cabin, (the original settlers on the lake), her sister Susie and brother-in-law Nick purchased a much valued piece of property towards the east end of the lake, a mile or so from us. The lake-front lot had been owned by the founder and long-time pastor of the church we had attended in Anchorage, and was part of the Joe DeWolfe homestead. Joe had worked at the military base as a power-plant operator, and had donated some of the property towards the expansion on the Abbott Loop Chapel building program.

After Nick cleared brush, and cut down the unnecessary and unwanted trees, I moved my air-rotary water well drilling rig onto the site, and drilled and located a wonderful tasting, clear water source that would supply a subdivision! The water source was in, but it had taken much longer to break-ground for the construction of the garage and building for living quarters, and the lot is sitting, partially undeveloped, waiting for the time of fruition.

Down on the point, sat an old log cabin that had been erected years ago, and it was there that Nick and Susie resided when on the property. A large fire pit was constructed to contain the comforting campfire while they watched the restful surroundings, sitting on the smooth flat surface of a bench made from a spruce log that had been split. The lot formed a small peninsula or point that stuck its nose out into Daniels Lake and usually caught a breeze, helping to keep the pesky mosquitoes at bay. The driveway was fairly steep, and somewhat paralleled the property line up-hill to the property's corner stake that had been driven into the ground, where the lot met the cul-de-sac at the top of the lot. On the opposite side of the driveway from the property line, toward the middle of their property stood a stately and mature white birch tree that for many years had battled the harsh winters, and being very hardy, had survived. I have heard of "Noble Fur Trees" but I would go "out on the limb" and call this a "Noble White Birch Tree", where the song birds found refuge, and made their nest to raise their young that would harvest the pesky mosquitoes and other insects that were a plague to mankind! Many times, ravens or magpies would sit high in the tree, scanning the area for a morsel of food for their young. This birch tree was well-grounded!

As you might have guessed, this was a special tree and very much appreciated and loved by the property owners. Nick had pruned the lower dead or dying limbs. After the house was constructed, they planned to build a swing to sit in the shade the tree offered.

The neighbor whose property joined Nick and Susie's lot, was doing a little clearing and wanted to help a good friend of his that had gained a few medals as he served proudly in the Armed Forces, and later worked and retired from a job in the lower forty-eight. He had recently migrated to Alaska from the sand and cactus and left Arnold in charge of the "hoards of illegal folks" swarming across the border. Settling on the Kenai, he had built a beautiful log home and was heating it with firewood. With all of the development now days, a person has to keep a sharp eye out for an area to harvest firewood!

Nick's neighbor and his Chechako friend were cutting some of the small birch trees that grew next to the property line. Nick's neighbor instructed his friend where to cut, and walked down the property line, and started thinning trees and brush in the lower section near the lake.

Just how long it was after Nick's neighbor walked to the lower end of the property, I do not know, but the

Chechako, as the old timers call new-comers, happen to look across the driveway of Nick and Susie's and spotted, standing alone, the tall, majestic white birch tree. The thought must have floated past his mind, "Now that is a tree that will heat the house for a long time!"

I do not know whether he was struck with a "Senior Moment", or maybe his brain "jumped out-of-gear, and slipped into neutral"! Paying no attention to the property line and the drive-way that separated the two lots, he carried his hungry chainsaw across the driveway and fired up his trusty Still, or Homelite, or what-ever brand he held, and proceeded to fell the majestic white birch tree. When Nick's neighbor noticed the tree leaning with the top quivering, and slowly at first, then faster, fall to the ground, blowing a dust cloud that would have choked a seasoned cattle-drive cowboy, he ran to the top of the hill in shock! He thought to himself! "WHAT DO I TELL NICK NOW!"

After much thinking about the situation, he called me on the phone and tried to explain what had happened, and asked if I could somehow "Break the news to Nick, GENTLY!" I couldn't believe my ears, at first, then reconciled to the facts, "- - it Happens!"

I was amazed at how God worked in this, as I expected Nick to literately "BLOW HIS STACK!", as I might have done! Nick in the past has demonstrated his strength by literally tearing an Anchorage Phone Book in half! As far as I know, his blood-pressure did not reach the point of him having a stroke! He seemed to take this all in stride, and did not harbor any animosity.

I must admit, I have had a "Senior Moment" in times past, when the brain seems to slip into "Neutral", and I can come up with no logical reason for my actions at the time! I think that might have happened to the Chechako, but……

MY ADVICE FOR THE FUTURE:
"NEVER LEAVE A CHECHAKO WITH A FUELED-UP CHAINSAW, UNLESS HE IS PICKETED TO HIS CUTTING AREA!"

"WELL, SHUT MY MOUTH!" AN OLD SOUTHERN SAYING THAT SHOULD BE ADHEARED TO MORE OFTEN

We were living in South Anchorage, on a lovely lot located on Avion Road with one and one-quarter acres of very usable land, only one block from the O'Malley Air Strip where I kept our Piper PA-18 Super Cub. In the summer we tilled a very preposterous garden which gave us a bounty of fresh vegetables, enough to enjoy ourselves, some to give-away to friends and family, and the excess to be pressure canned or blanched and frozen and placed into the thirty-one cubic foot freezer. In the back portion of the property, I had fenced off a section to coral our four horses that we used for pleasure riding and also for a small Packing and Outfitting Business, taking hunters and adventurers into the Alaskan wilds.

The main occupation and the only true source of income was our water-well drilling, pump sales and service business, "Vern's Drilling and Enterprises". Once, when asked why the "and Enterprises" on the business title. I replied, "It gives me a Long Tail to Wag!" I had ventured into other business ideas, but none of those became a via-able source of the much needed "Green-Backs".

I had never had a large enough shop to get my drill equipment into for maintenance and repair, and have worked outside in the sub-zero, or the rainy weather, lying on a piece of card-board or plywood to insulate my body from the cold or wet ground. A friend from the church we attended had bid on and bought a huge metal building at an auction on the local military base. He had no use for all of the building, so "separated unto himself" a section to erect a garage at his home-site. The remaining, and larger section of the building, he offered to sell to me. I thought about it, and drove to the location of the building materials, which proved to be extremely good quality, very heavy gauge galvanized metal, extremely strong design, and should be relatively simple to erect.

My wife Sharon never really cared for the look of the building, as it was like building a coliseum in front of a "summer cottage", the thing was so huge! Well, "the Proof of the pudding is in the Tasting, not what it looks like!" It did give an appearance of "Being out of Place?" But it would give me lots of room to work in.

The shop building had the roof in place, a huge sliding door in the front, and a man-door in the rear near my office door of our house. I was installing the long and heavy galvanized ceiling panels, and Sharon's cousin Larry, who had moved up from

Minnesota with his family, had volunteered to help me.

Now Larry had been a "Timber Cruiser" in Minnesota after a stint in the Marines, serving in Vietnam, and then attending college to get his "Forestry Degree". Larry had been interested in many of the things I had done when I came to Alaska: working on the first oil Pipeline to the Swanson River, becoming an Operating Engineer running heavy equipment road building: trapping and hunting, running a dog team and with my trapping-partner Jay, operating the first Arctic Cat Snowmachine on the Kenai Peninsula: training and entering a dog in the Anchorage Fur Rendezvous Weight Pull Contest and winning and setting a new record: running a horse-back Packing and Outfitting business: running river boats: commercial fishing as skiff-man on a Prince William Sound Purse Seine boat: buying a Super Cub airplane and reviving instruction for my pilot's license and Bush Flying all over the state of Alaska, hunting and fishing: just to mention a few things. I could go on, but we will save on the ink for now!

Larry loved to read, and he gleaned quite a bit from the books. He also was endowed with an abundance of energy, and if you were to give him a steel-handled axe, you had better have him chained off to a steel post, or he might cut the whole forest down! If the axe had a wood-handle, the forest might be safe! The political arena missed out when he decided against being a Politician", as he loved a good argument or debate. Larry later worked and retired from a position of a Corrections Officer for the State of Alaska. One thing at work, if he were to get into a debate with an inmate, at least he had "a captive audience". And as the politicians love to spend other people's money, he loved to give me "suggestions and advice as what I should do", and among the suggestions was for me to start my own dog kennel, train the dogs and "Run the Iditarod Race!" This, he said, running the Iditarod would be the adventure of a life-time! Yes, I must agree with him. But more than an adventure, it is a "Heck of a Long and Cold Camping Trip!" Unless you were in the lead, you might be dodging dog poop the whole way! I had given it some thought at one time, but "I had too much on my plate" at present, and no time to raise a dog team. Besides, I've slept on the frozen ground long enough to earn fifty or more "Merit Badges in Cold Weather Camping."

We were working away, straining with the long and cold galvanized panels that we held over-head, and with the frost clinging to our coat collars and mustaches as it build up with all the moist and heated discussion. I knew Larry thought he would love to enter the Iditarod Race, but many times when a person is actually partaking of the event, they realize what work and drudgery it can be. This is probably when the expression, "ARE WE HAVING FUN YET?" might have originated!

Finally, I had enough of the suggestion of me entering the Iditarod Race. I stopped the work at hand, and looked him in the eye and said, "Larry, if you want to run the Iditarod Race so bad, all you have to do is get your own dog team or rent one and go for it. I said, "ALL YOU NEED IS THE 'BALLS' TO JUST DO IT!" Larry did not mention the Iditarod again that evening!

Well, time has flown by, and there has been a lot of water flow under the bridge. It seems I've Never Learned to "Keep My Big Mouth Shut!" It seems that I just, 'Open my mouth: Insert my Foot!"

The year was 1985, and Libby Riddles left the boys behind in the warmth of their shelter and braved the fierce storm, slept on the trail during the roaring blizzard, and won the Iditarod Race. And that proved me wrong! "You Didn't Need the ATTACHMENTS, after-all!"

As a side note: When we saw Larry and his wife, at the 2009 family Christmas party in Anchorage, he called me aside and said I needed to get started on a book with some of my experiences and stories. "If you don't, I'm going to start writing some of them and publish a book and I'll get the money!" For years, my wife, daughters, and many friends had been after me to get some of the stories on paper or a "voice recorder". Well, it's March 4, 2010, lots of snow on the ground, and I'm working at it!

When I Play Marbles, I Play For Keeps!

During the 1970's, while attending Abbott Loop Christian Center in Anchorage, I had a friend, Jack Marrow, who was the Head of the South-central Alaska Highways Commission. It seemed the state needed to drill a water well in Takotna, Alaska. Now the Takotna job was not your everyday "pack a sack lunch, load the service truck and drill rig, and drive to the drilling site" type job. Takotna lies west of Denali along the world famous Iditarod Trail, about Mile 369, and is located in the Kilbuck-Kuskokwim Mountains, and on the north bank of the Takotna River. The Alaska Department of Highways building sat on top of a hill overlooking the village and the Takotna River, a beautiful location to say the least. Down in the village, some of the cabins had hand driven sand-points to supply water. A sand-point is a pointed steel pipe about two to three feet in length with slots along its side to allow water to be drawn into the pipe. It is driven into the soil with a sledge hammer or other means of driving, sections of pipe are added, and then driven down into the hopefully shallow surface water. A suction pump, either a hand type pump or a motor powered is then attached to the upper pipe, water is poured into the pump to prime it, and the stroking begins. As the pump handle is stroked up and down, the water is sucked into the pipe and discharges water at the pump outlet on top.

As an example, where my wife Sharon and I live in the former home of Earl and Florence Daniels, located north of Kenai, AK, on Daniels Lake, the original water system was a hand driven one and one quarter inch galvanized pipe, with a bronze sand-point threaded onto the front or lead section, and driven with a sledge hammer to a depth of about fifteen feet into the water zone and was below the level of the lake out in front of the cabin. In front of the sink, a throw rug could be moved aside to expose a floor board that could be removed to make accessible a six foot deep "cellar" or basement under the floor, where the pipe came up from the ground. Along the edge of this excavation a few boards had been laid down and canned food or any other food that needed to be kept cool was placed. The pipe came up from the ground and then penetrated the kitchen floor and extended through the sink counter where a small hand-operated Suction Pump was mounted on the counter, at the edge of the sink. As the pump handle was stroked, the water was sucked into the lower screened end of the pipe and up and discharged into the sink. What a blessing that was by not having to go out to the frozen lake and cut a hole in the three feet deep ice to scoop up a bucket of water and carry it to the cabin. The lake water sometimes carried traces of the decomposed red salmon that had spawned and died in the lake. In the fall, a person had to row well out into the lake, to get away from the bank and keep the slime and particles of the decomposing salmon out of the drinking water bucket.

Well, Jack wanted to hire me to "Contract Labor" the job of drilling the water well for the state. The State of Alaska Department of Highways would lease an old track mounted Bucyrus-Armstrong cable tool drill from Mr. O'Carroll, a gold miner in Ophir, which is about eighteen to twenty miles away along the old gravel road that had been used during the "Gold Mining Days". This was a "Churn Drill", a percussion drill or "Pounder" as some called it. This is a slow way of drilling, especially if you encountered bedrock or large cobbles or boulders. Any way you look at it, it was hard, slow work.

After a few days, Jack phoned me and said they had the Bucyrus-Armstrong drill moved to Takotna, and were ready for me to fly out. On July 14, 1975, Gary, the pilot who I had worked with at Interior Airways from 1968 to 1970, flew me over in a chartered Sea Air Motive Cessna 206 aircraft. I loaded my gear into a couple of duffel bags, and also took a "sand pump bailer" a tool I had fabricated a few years before.

Jack had come along to help get things started. Dave, the superintendent of the Takotna operation had told Jack about some old dynamite that needed to be destroyed. As Jack was a State of Alaska Licensed Powder man he was legal to do the work and located the old dynamite and with it resting on a soft cloth, sat in the back of the pickup truck with me as we rode towards the local dump. Jack properly burned the explosive while I rode out to Ophir to the gold miner's location to get a set of drive blocks to attach to the drill stem and for driving the six inch steel casing into the ground. Later when I was working with the drill, Jack asked if I needed some help. I said I had rather work alone, unless I could get some good help! He then told me a mutual friend Allen G. now worked for the state, and he could send him over to help. Well, I knew Allen to be a top notch worker, equipment friendly and pretty easy to get along with. I said I would be thankful to him if he could get Allen. Otherwise, I'd work alone.

July 18, 1975, Allen's Cessna 206 flight landed at the small airstrip on top of the hill, just out of town. He was transported to Dave's house where

the front room was used as the office.
Allen came in, and as it was raining
and late in the day, we decided to wait
until the next morning to start the
drill rig again. We were having coffee
and talking things over when in came
two local boys, rather tall and very
"Skookum" or Robust looking. They both
had bruises and scars on their faces, a
tooth or two missing in front, and
really looked tough. They were talking
to Dave, and finally looked over
towards Allen and me, and said, "What I
like to do is get drunked up, and come
and whip-up on the new white man in
town!" They smiled and looked at each
other, both agreeing on the "whip up on
the new white man in town idea". I
just sat there, not saying anything and
was thinking the whole thing over. I
am definitely not Albert Einstein, but
this math problem was not that hard to
figure out! Allen's airplane was the
last plane into town, and my plane had
come just before his, so I guessed they
might be talking about whipping up on
us! We sat there while they laughed
and told of kicking the "stuffing" and
"other matter" out of a few white men
that had come to Takotna. Finally I
thought I had better interject a few
facts of my own.

I figured Allen could take care
of himself, but with two bucks their
size; it would be a real job for
anyone. I had been in an automobile

accident and was a passenger on the right side of the vehicle. At mile seven, Old Seward Highway, a black driver who was sparking some young gal, was looking across the road at something, or had his hands off the steering-wheel, but surely not paying attention to his driving, and swerved into our lane and hit us head-on. The seat broke loose on my side and I was thrown forward, driving me into the dash where I immediately tried to devour the foam on the dash. Three of my front teeth were knocked out, with one dangling by the nerve, ooooooooooweeee! That HURT! I had to have two root cannels and three teeth replaced. I think if I could have reached the old boy driving the car that hit us, he would not have had to explain to his wife what he was doing with this young gal in the front seat of the car! Instead, he would have been pushing up posies and his family would be singing some of his favorite songs.

Now, back in Takotna, we watched the local bucks show the size of their fists, grinning and telling of what they would do, finally I spoke up. "Boys, I've had too much dental work to enjoy boxing anymore. If you want to play with me, I play marbles for keeps!" As was my custom, I was wearing a vest. I pulled the left side of the new brown Carhartt vest aside to expose the custom fitted walnut grips of a six inch barreled, stainless steel, Model 629 Smith and Wesson .44 Remington Magnum, that when gripped, became an extension of my arm. I had traced the outline of my fingers onto the walnut grip and had cut grooves with a rat-tail file to fit my fingers perfectly. This was one of the most comfortable pistols I have ever fired, and I had run hundreds of rounds through it. I knew it well!

I stroked the walnut grip of the .44 Magnum and said, "Now Boys, when you come, I want you coming in a straight line, and four in a row. I shoot hard cast 250 grain bullets and I know damned well I can take four of you at a time!"

The smirks and grimaces faded from their faces like chalk drawings on a rain swept sidewalk. I gently pulled the vest back, covering the Smith and Wesson that was cradled in the Lawrence Quick-Draw shoulder holster, and I gave them a friendly smile. Time Stood Still! The only sound being made was the hiss of the tea kettle on the oil fire stove.

I don't remember if it was crocheting, needle work, or golf, but the subject changed! The smirk, the hard eyes, and the mean smiles were gone from their faces. They then began to smile friendly toward us.

155

The glare was gone from their eyes. Allen and I smiled and nodded to the two scared faced boys and we were friends from that time forward! From that moment forward, each time we spotted the boys in town or anywhere else they always smiled from ear to ear and gave us a big friendly wave. It is amazing what a little "Authority" will do!

The drill-line cable on the rig was very old and brittle and broke on us, and we lost the tool down the hole. We went to Ophir to O'Carroll's place to borrow a tool to recover the drill-stem tool. No such luck. Later, I took a piece of casing and cut it down with an oxygen and acetylene torch and made a Horn-socket fishing tool, and Praise the Lord, it worked well enough that we were able to get the drill tool out. We ordered new cable and replaced the old one and had no more trouble breaking off.

At around seventy feet, we started hitting decomposed bedrock, and a little "color" or very fine gold flakes! When the "cuttings" or ground-up bits of rock were removed from the well, you could see a hint of fine gold. Well, why not! This area is noted for the gold mining! I wish now, we had located a gold pan, and tried to recover some of the fine gold. We drilled to a total depth of ninety feet and it was all bedrock from seventy five feet down. There was a small amount of water coming in from fractures in the bedrock, and there was some water just above the bedrock, but now held back by the steel casing that was driven into the bedrock. I called Jack and had him order enough Explosive Stick-Jet casing perforators (explosive charges to shoot holes in the steel pipe and let the water come in), and also detonation cord, electric blasting caps, and a roll of shooting wire to connect the blasting-cap to the surface to detonate the explosives. These were purchased from my friend and later to be hunting partner, Buck Kuhn of Statewide Blasting and Perforating Service.

Buck had instructed me in the safe use of dynamite and the explosive perforators while we blasted a few wells together in earlier years. Allen and I had no trouble making up the charges, lowering them into the well to the desired location and used the battery of the drill rig to detonate the charges and shoot holes in the steel casing well pipe. It always got the attention of the town folks when we shot off a charge! After explosive perforating the casing, we cleaned and removed the debris from the well. We finally had the well drilling completed and folded the Bucyrus-Armstrong drill rig to the "travel" position. With this job completed, I informed Jack we were ready to get back to town.

July 25, 1975, a Sea Air Motive turbo Beaver on floats landed in the river in front of town, loaded our gear, and gave Allen and me a ride to Anchorage. As the pilot taxied out and then "fire-walled the engine", we waved good bye to the people of Takotna, and especially to the two new friends we had acquired, both with missing front teeth, and big smiles on their bruised and scarred faces. Hands waving!

"Who was it that said, "Walk softly and carry a big stick?" I actually prefer my Smith and Wesson.

"WHILE WE ARE SPEAKING OF EXPLOSIVES"
THE LOW IQ TERRORIST

The fellow who started the "Hot Foot Terrorist Society" by trying to set off a bomb hidden in his "tenny-runners" aboard a major airline flight wasn't too savvy when it came to explosives. It appears his tennis shoe bomb in actuality turned out to be no more than a "One-time-use Emergency Foot Warmer!" But it did get the security folks on the ball, and now most people wash their feet before a flight, at least for the large commercial airlines. It is slowly catching on with the locals!

HOT CROTCH CHRISTMAS BOMBER WITH THE LOW I-Q

Comments on the Hot Crotch Bomber of Christmas Airplane Flight 2009: The Security Folks really screwed up by not doing an in-depth "Haines or Huggie" search on that fellow. Coming from the region of the world where many terrorists are hatched, it should have been "a no brainier" for the Security Folks at the airport, to look him over very closely, especially after his father went to the authorities before hand and informed them of his other than "Boy Scout" activities and his political ideas. It seems that he had received training "in the do it yourself making of

159

bombs, and other explosives, and their handy use in bringing down airliners, trains, or other vehicles".

Apparently his trainers didn't differentiate between detonating an explosive and "safely destroying" an explosive. The Would-be Terrorist could have used a Roy Rogers Deluxe Model Cap-Pistol and held it to his exposed crotch and rapidly fired the cap pistol and caused the explosive material to go off with a "BOOM"! He merely (unknowingly) followed the last section of the book on how to safely dispose of explosives material, by simply burning it. I bet he had a "HOT PAIR OF HAINES", or he "Baked his Fruit of the Looms" after he "Flicked his Bic" in that confined area.

Fortunately the Airport Security people weren't the only "dummies" that day!

It always seems that the foolish actions of a few "dumb bells" or "no goods" causes more restrictions to be imposed on the mass of folk that are trying to be honest and not harm their neighbor. I think we need a "Caning Law" (Public Spanking) here in the good old USA! It's amazing how a little "Pain" gets a person's attention! Just placing them into a prison that resembles a "Health Club" has little or no effect on them!

PRIDE COMETH BEFORE A FALL! YOU CAN BET YOUR BOOTS ON IT!

We were hunting along the Denali Highway in one of our "Secret Hunting Spots" north of the major river of the area, and were geared up for meat gathering in the highest sense. After driving two pick-up trucks towing four horse trailers each with riding saddles, pack saddles, tents, camping gear, horse food, pistols, knives, and rifles from the Anchorage area, we let the horses out on long picket ropes to graze while we built a fire and cooked a few vittles for ourselves. The horses now limbered up, we saddled and loaded the panniers and pack bags, top packed the sleeping bags and tent, mounted our trusty steeds and made our way to the river, carefully chose a crossing spot and made the crossing without getting the gear or ourselves wet! On the north bank of the mountain we located a sheltered camping spot with golden canopy of the aspen trees, dissected by a small stream that we used for drinking and cooking. As usual, the first night away from home, we didn't sleep very well, tossed and turned on our two inch thick LL Bean Trail Bed foam mattress that was separated from the cold and damp ground by a thin tarp.

For breakfast, we had fried thick-sliced bacon, fried cackle berries (also known as eggs), bread toasted on a stick over the fire, generously coated with real butter and orange marmalade spread thick! This was washed down with plenty of strong black coffee by me, the boys had to add about a quarter cup of sugar and the same amount of canned milk to get theirs down. The horses had been grained and were saddled and carried light pack bags and panniers with clean cotton game bags, to protect the moose meat we would soon harvest! Nothing like confidence! We mounted and rode away from camp with me bringing up the rear leading a pack horse and soon approached a fast running stream with steep banks on both sides.

The boys were trying to coax their trusty steeds to cross the fast moving mountain stream, but to no avail! Buck was kicking the ribs of his Appaloosa horse so hard, the horse was wringing his short tail in a circle and was passing gas so fast, it sounded like an air rifle going off! Finally, he reined his horse aside and back up the hill out of the way to let Terry lead the way across the stream. Terry's horse was a high spirited, prancer and head shaker and wanted nothing to do with the fast moving water, and was throwing his head so high he almost hit Terry in the face, with the reins flapping the air. Finally, I had had enough and called out, "If you boys will step aside, I'll show you how to cross this stream!" Terry reined his high-spirited steed aside, and I gently nudged the sorrel colored registered Quarter-horse with my spurs, not jabbing, but letting him know to move ahead. He shuffled his way down the steep bank, loose gravel rolling ahead and into the creek, placed his front feet into the water, slowly turned his head and looked at me, as if asking if he could partake of the refreshing water at his feet. I eased the reins forward to let him know it was alright to get a drink. The first mistake of the day!

Chips, as my horse was called, front feet were in the creek, but his back feet were about two feet higher, still on the steep slope of the bank. As he lowered his head to get a drink, I felt the saddle start sliding forward. I should have jerked his head up, but I didn't want to get rough with him. Mistake number two!

Although very old, the saddle I was using was new to me, and had originally been used in Montana, probably before Charles Russell came to that country. With smooth leather seat, cantle about six and one half inches high, pommel very high and wide, it was a bucking horse saddle of the old days. When a person climbed into that saddle, they needed a pry-bar or "sky hoist" to get you out! As this

Quarter Horse had a narrow wither I had placed two blankets on his back before installing the old Montana saddle. I tightened up the single-shot cinch (only one cinch strap located in the center on the saddle) and loaded my leather saddle bags behind the saddle, tied them on with the leather thongs of the saddle, shoved my rifle into the leather scabbard that was attached to the saddle, and climbed aboard, so comfortable a person could easily fall asleep and not fall out of this "rocking-chair"!

Have you ever smelled the "musky smell" of a scared animal? I was beginning to omit that "Scared Musky Smell" while wedged in the tight seat of the saddle, sliding forward, over the withers of the horse, and looking down into the fast moving water strewn with boulders! "What a Mell of a Hess!" as my Dad used to say! I tried to stand as "tall in the saddle" as I could, while leaning back to stop the forward movement of the saddle, but to no avail! With one hand held upward to cushion my head first fall into the cold mountain stream, I tried to grab a handful of horse mane, but to no avail. Buck said my butt looked like the "sun setting in the west" as it disappeared from sight. "SPLASH", I hit the water head first, wrinkling the four inch brim of my brown Bandera hat. I was immediately covered with ice cold water, got up as quickly as I could, and ran to catch the two saddle blankets that were now floating swiftly downstream. Walked to a gravel bar nearby, tossed the blankets down and went back to the horse that was still standing in the rigging! I pushed him aside and drug the saddle with saddle bags, rifle scabbard containing a Belgium made Browning Safari Grade .308 Norma rifle with Leupold scope to the island and dropped them onto the gravel. The boys were laughing so hard I thought they might fall out of their saddles! What a sight! My red and black checkered Pendleton wool coat had water flowing from it as if it were being recharged by a fire hydrant! I sat down, removed my cowboy boots with spurs, and poured about a half gallon of water from each one, and finally had a good laugh over the spill myself! It does not pay to get "Cocky" and Proverbs 16:18 came to my mind, "Pride goes before destruction, a haughty spirit before a fall." So True! I was now standing about two inches shorter due to the compaction of my neck and spine! Looks like I'll never catch up with John Wayne!

I led Chips to the gravel bar and tied him to a willow tree, shook out the blankets, replaced them onto his back, and re-saddled the horse. Knowing there would be trouble if I could not come up with a breeching

strap or something to keep the saddle
from going forward as we rode downhill, thought for a moment, and an idea
came to me. I removed a rope from my
saddle bag, ran it around Chip's tail
at the base and tied a bowline loop,
then ran the other end of the rope
under the saddle on top of the blanket,
forward underneath the saddle and up at
the saddle horn, and made a couple of
half hitches. This should work fine!
Re-mounting my horse, and we proceeded
up the long hill toward the base of the
mountain where we were to hunt.
Everything went fine until we had a
slight dip to cross, and started
downhill. The saddle moved forward,
the loop around the base of Chip's tail
tightened, he slowly raised his head
and turned to look toward his tail! He
thought for sure something was about to
get him, snorted, and began to buck! I
was wedged into the saddle so
comfortably he stood no chance of
dumping me. After a few crow-hops, I
reined him in and took control and we
eased our way up the valley and stopped
on the sunny southern slope with
blueberry patch. There I stretched out
on the soft moss and let the sun do its
evaporation work on the wet clothes.

A little hint thrown in here! I
was wearing wool pants, shirt, and
coat. Wool has the properties that
keep you warm, even when the garments
are wet! The only time I was really

cold was when I was actually in the mountain stream, but started warming up as soon as I walked out of the water. Think about the good properties of wool, may cost a bit more, but wool can save your life in a bad situation! It saved my bacon a time or two!

While glassing the valley below, we spotted a small "mulligan moose" as we call them. They are not big enough to be a trophy, but make a heck of a mulligan stew! Terry wanted the moose if possible, so Buck decided to go along and be his back-up man. I would remain on the hill and eat blueberries and soaking up sunshine, continue to dry out, while keeping watch on the horses. The boys checked their rifles, and began their long walk to where the mulligan moose was "mowing" willows down near a berry covered hill with dwarf willow patches bordering the clear mountain stream that divided the valley. I witnessed their pussy-footing around the brush trying to get into position for Terry to shoot the moose, which disappeared and so did the boys. After a few minutes, I heard the "BOOM" of a rifle and soon saw one of the boys walk into view, and motion me to come down by waving his cowboy hat.

After tightening my saddle's cinch strap, I gathered and eased the horses down toward the kill site and what a surprise! While stalking the moose, a beautiful eight foot grizzly bear minding his own business, eating blueberries behind the hill was spotted. Buck decided to take him, did a sneak and shot him behind the ear, closing the last chapter of his life. Now, while hanging on the wall, the open-mouth-rug mounted bear with long shinning claws stands guard over Buck's office.

Terry later in the week, shot a moose, and I also shot a seven foot plus grizzly bear, and had to go into the brush after him. When spotted, the grizzly was grazing down in the valley with about seventy yards or more of thick alder bushes between us. As there was no way to make a quiet stalk on him, I got into a sitting position and shot for his spine. The first shot was just below the spine, allowing him to run into the brush. Exciting time as I went in after him, with Buck standing rifle in hand on a hummock about twenty yards away, ready to shoot the bear off me if need be. Creeping around a patch of buck-brush, I found him nose down in the tundra. The .308 Norma Magnum's 200 grain Bitterroot Bonded Core Bullet had done its' job.

FLYING OVER "SATAN'S SANDBOX"
"BOB HANSEN'S KILLING GROUND"

In September of 1980, my wife and I were able to purchase a used Piper PA-18A aircraft, 8081 Charlie, a "Flat-Back" or "Crop Duster" model. The spray rigging had been removed, but the large "Hopper Door" was still on the back. When flying to a remote area and carrying lots of supplies, I always loaded her "to the hilt" and then opened the hopper door, and placed the bread and eggs up there, where it would not get crushed. She had the Atlee Dodge "Extended Baggage" compartment, and was a real joy to fly.

After purchasing 8081 Charlie, I started using the Knik River area again. But this time as a practice area for my Super Cub and a place to take visitors and view wildlife, as you could almost always spot moose, bear, sheep and goats in the upper valley.

There was an area between the New Glenn Highway bridge and the Old Glenn Highway bridge along the Knik River where there were hundreds of acres of flat sand bars on which to practice "bush landings". In some areas, there were tall cottonwood trees, spruce trees, willow and alder thickets tall grass and almost any condition you could imagine to practice the slow, full-flap, extremely short field landing and take-off required to successfully bush fly in Alaska. Each spring, a few of us "Bush Pilot" friends would go up to the Knik River sand-bars, mark off a two hundred foot area, and practice landing in this spot, and then taking off from the same area. The long sand bars allowed a person to fly very low and slow on approach without the danger of crashing if we came down too soon. We have made some very "bumpy landings" when first practicing, after a long spell without doing the "short-field" work.

Another thing we did in this area was, test and experiment with different standard tires and "Tundra Tires" to see which offered the most flotation in the soft sand, softness when landing (absorb the bumps and roughness of the terrain) and the short-field performance when taking off. After practicing enough to get "the Feel" back, we would sometimes fly up and down the area, and looking for small islands in the river, just long enough to land and stop on, if your skills were in "Top Shape". Most of these islands were just a few hundred feet long, and if you made a mistake, you would end up in the river! It sure kept the adrenaline flowing!

On our trips up to the Knik River sand bars and on up to Lake George, we usually knew most of the few airplanes we might encounter. Occasionally you spotted one you did not know. It was on one occasion I spotted a Piper Super Cub that had landed on a narrow sand bar in a timbered area, and had a small "Pop Tent" erected just in front of the engine and right wing. I thought it strange for someone who owned an airplane to be "Camping this close to town", and the idea that "Someone Is Cheating on his wife" came to my mind. I did not recognize the plane at that time, and flew on up river towards Lake George. Upon my return home, I noticed the plane and tent were still there. The "Cheating was still in progress!" Little did I know how "Horrifying the Cheating Was!"

A year or so later, my hunting partner Buck and I noticed a small cove near this spot where I had seen the Super Cub and "Pop Tent" campsite, and it looked as if a herd of "Amateur Clam Diggers" were practicing, or someone with a "New Metal Detector" and shovel had been at work there looking for "Gold Doubloons". The area was littered with shallow "Dig Holes" or "Pock Marks" in the smooth sandy surface. Little did I know of the "Gruesome Events" that had taken place in this section of the Knik

River floodplain. This was "Satan's Sandbox" for sure!

November 29, 1984, my friend and hunting partner Buck called from Ft Worth, Texas, and said he had located a used Cessna 182 and asked if I would help him fly the plane to Alaska. This I agreed to, and purchased items he could not find in Texas, such as an insulated engine cover, a set of wing covers, and cold weather gear needed for the cold trip north. After waiting for the needed repairs to radio systems, we made the trip to Alaska without getting "Frost Bite". Along the way we met some very friendly and special folks during our frequent "Lay-over" while waiting for the weather to clear or warm up a bit. Much of the trip was well below zero temperature.

The following spring, Buck had purchased wide "Tundra Tires" for the Cessna 182 and was testing them up on the Knik River sand bars, and landed and taxied to a spot with very soft sand, not far from where I had previously seen the Super Cub and "Pop Tent" in the "Suspicious Camping Area".

While there, he noticed a beautiful flower, standing by its self, and walked over to examine it. At the base of the flower stem was the exposed bone that a fox had dug up and had been chewing on. Buck picked up the bone to examine it, and saw it resembled the "fore-arm" bone of a small human. After reading and viewing all of the newspaper accounts and television media accounts, he realized this area had been used by the serial killer Bob Hansen. Buck walked back to the airplane, retrieved his shovel, and went back for a closer examination. A few inches back from the exposed bone, he came upon pinkish-red decomposed human flesh, and a blanket. He realized what he had stumbled upon, and after reaching his home he called the State Troopers and notified them of his findings, and later showed them the gravesite.

After reading of Bob Hansen's arrest in 1983, I felt sure Bob Hansen was the pilot of the Super Cub and the owner of the "Pop Tent". Now, after Buck discovered the last burial site to be located, my theory was again fortified. The Super Cub and "Pop Tent" belonged to Bob Hansen, the serial killer of many young women who were working as strippers and prostitutes, whom Bob had lured into his vehicle and kidnapped, raped and later brutally killed. And for all its closeness to Anchorage, Eagle River, Chugach, and small communities along the way, the area was remote enough so as not to be visible to the traveler along a roadway. Much of the area had to be accessed by boat, airplane, all terrain vehicle, or hiking.

As a bonus to its relatively easy access and the closeness to civilization; the traveler with something to hide, be it a treasure or be it incriminating evidence against himself, the Knik River has worked in his favor. For over the years, the rain and the snow and the waters of the Knik River have cleaned the sand so well, there was very little "binder" (clay, loam, hardpan, etc.) in the fine sand, and it is extremely easy to excavate!

The animals that call this area their home, have also helped in disposing of incriminating evidence, be it a poached moose or sheep or other animal, or even the remains of an unfortunate human being.

This area could well be called, "Satan's Sand Box", for surly evidence of Satan's influence has been manifested here!

I DID NOT KNOW HIM WELL

The first time I remember meeting Bob Hansen was in the late 1960's when I had a small gun shop in the basement of our log home located on Eagle Street, between Northern Lights Blvd. and Fireweed Street, in Anchorage. My wife and I had purchased the small cabin about a year or so after being married in 1964, and a three-sided log addition on a concrete block full basement was added. With the concrete work done by myself, the floor was "rough as a cob". Reloading supplies, were sold (the favorite item was bulk 4831 rifle powder which I purchased in the 100 pound keg and the buyer brought his own container). Also stocked were pack boards, used firearms, and a few new rifles and pistols, but with limited finances for expansion, the shop closed in 1970, and as summer approached, I hired on as "skiff-man" on a purse seine boat during a very poor fishing year, and after cutting and selling firewood, January of 1971, entered the water well drilling industry.

At the time of opening the gun shop, I was working at Interior Airways (later named Mark Air) with a few friends that migrated there after going on strike at Reeve Aleutian Airways, and a settlement was never reached. Just before we walked out on strike, the owner Bob Reeve, known as the "Glacier Pilot", walked out into the hanger where a few of us were working on a DC-6 airplane. We had voted to "go on strike" within a few days, and he warned us, "Boys, it's going to be a Long Cold Winter", and was he right! It was a very long and cold winter and the finances were very low!

My good friend Atlee Dodge Jr. and I had constructed a sign using heavy aluminum with the painting of a rifle and the words, "Vern's Shooting Supplies". This hung below our mail box out front and served us well. The shop's entrance was in the rear of the building with steps down to a large wooden door. I remember when Bob Hansen, unknown to me at the time, came in and stood at the door. I greeted him from behind my glass show-case counter and told him to help himself and look around. I resumed working on the wood rifle stock I was "glass-bedding" to make the rifle shoot more accurately. Bob looked around for awhile, and then walked to the door and left without saying much at all. I don't know if he shoplifted anything or not.

I later saw Bob Hansen at a small "Sportsmen's Show" at the church my family was attending, but I do not recall ever seeing him at any of the regular meetings. I had a small display with some good moose and trophy caribou antlers and photos of our horse packing and outfitting trips, etc. They were good, but nothing spectacular.

On the contrary, Bob Hansen had some of the mounted trophy class heads of Dall sheep he had entered into the record books. As a testimony of their products, "Herters World Famous Outfitters" catalog featured a photo or two of Bob Hansen in his living room with some of his trophies, many taken with "Herters brand" archery products.

I, for some unknown reason, never felt comfortable around him, and did not try to be a friend to him. A couple of my friends from church tried to reach out to him, one offering him help at his bakery, which he refused. My other friend and his wife visited Bob and his wife at their home. I remember my friend telling of the strange look in Bob's eyes as he told of shooting "marmots" (rodents similar to groundhog or woodchuck that live in the mountains) up near the Devils Creek cabin of the Resurrection Trail area. My friend stated how Bob held the small caliber rifle to his shoulder, and sighting at an invisible target, snapped the trigger, cocked the rifle again, moved the barrel slightly to sight onto another invisible target, and snap the trigger

again. This went on until at least
seven or eight invisible targets were
shot. All the while, Bob staring in
deep concentration at the invisible
targets, as if he was reliving each
"kill". My friend said Bob appeared
very "strange" in the manner which he
relived the "marmot hunts". I doubt
if he were visualizing "marmots" in
his sights!

WHATEVER IT TAKES

"What Ever It Takes" was an expression used by a flying instructor in Alaska, now gone to the "Sweet Bye and Bye". When asked what to do in a given situation to keep from stalling the airplane or crashing or just ground-looping, his reply was "What Ever It Takes!" That is a mental attitude more of us need to acquire in life. When we are faced with circumstances that are not to our liking, we need to do "What Ever It Takes" to survive the moment and keep on going on with life!

February 27, 1984, I was sitting at the kitchen table enjoying a strong cup of black coffee, after the evening meal of moose-meat Swiss steak, thick milk-gravy, boiled spuds, all liberally coated with "black pepper to keep the flies off", and canned sweet corn. The phone rang, and when I answered it, I was greeted by a very anxious and worried lady, a friend and the wife of a fellow aviator from O'Malley Air Strip where I kept our Piper Super Cub tied down. My friend Dan, who flew an Interstate airplane on skis during the winter, had been returning with a friend as passenger from a caribou hunting trip near the Mulchatna River area, on the west side of Cook Inlet and the Aleutian Range. She had received a message that had been forwarded by an air-taxi operator from Lake Hood in Anchorage, Dan and his friend had made an emergency landing near the Little Susitna River, and badly needed assistance. His message to her was, "Call Vern!" "I'll get into the air as soon as it was light enough to see in the morning" was my reply.

My sleep that night was not the best, as I ran scenario after scenario through my mind thinking of what might have happened. And as it usually is best not to think of every problem that may await you, I was finally able to get a few hours of rest. Finally morning, I had fried caribou Polish sausage, fried spuds, toast and two "cackle-berries" over easy, for breakfast. I filled my thermos with hot black coffee, and threw into a small knapsack, a couple of packages of smoked salmon and moose summer sausage, and a box of "Pilot Bread" for snacking on later in the day. Before leaving the house, I placed the red metal Eagle brand gas can which contained the engine oil drained from my Super Cub's engine after the last flight, onto the gas burner of our cook stove. The oil would be heated to near boiling and later poured into the pre-heated Lycoming 150 HP engine before starting it. This way, the engine received immediate lubrication, instead of the bearings running dry while the cold and thick oil could be forced threw the oil passages! The "Cold Starts" accounted for many of the pilots having a very short engine life! I always was able to get the full recommended hours on my engines before overhaul!

It was still dark when I parked my Ford Crew Cab 4x4 truck in front of the little red and white PA-18 Super Cub with the nylon wing and engine covers to ward off the frost from its flying surfaces. I fired the 12 volt, propane fueled engine heater and installed the four inch pipe conducting the heat under the cowling and went about with my "Preflight" inspection before flying. With the engine heated enough I could easily rotate the long Boar Prop, without "chinning myself on it", I poured in the hot engine oil, primed the engine with gasoline, I rotated the propeller four turns to "load gasoline to each cylinder", and turned the left magneto to the "On Position". With the engine primed and ready, I advanced the throttle forward all the way, then back to the stop and one-half inch forward. I stood on the ski and was behind the prop when I reached forward and "snapped" the prop down, and was rewarded with the roar of the engine, gently "looping". The right magneto was then switched to the on position and the engine smoothed out, purring like a kitten!

With the truck moved out of the way, I removed the wing covers and stuffed them into the red nylon bag and placed it into the rear of the Cub as it gently quivered from side to side as the engine tried to pull forward. Everything in a go position, I untied the rope restraining the tail ski, crawled into the plane, secured the wide "Crop Duster" seat belt and shoulder harness, placed the David Clark headset with boom mike on my head and turned the radio on, announced my intentions, and taxied onto the runway, and to the north end near the hill with the tall spruce trees. With a blast of power, I "blew" the tail of the plane around and faced down the long snow covered runway, and keyed the mike switch which was located on my control stick, similar to a trigger on a rifle. "O'Malley air traffic, 4302 Zulu departing on the runway south, O'Malley Air Strip!"

The throttle was slowly advanced forward to the firewall and within a few yards, reached down with my left hand and pulled the flap lever to the full position and the little plane leaped into the air! If you have never been able to fly a good Piper PA-18 Super Cub that is rigged correctly, you have missed one of the joys of life! Many of the small bush planes are fun to fly, but flying a PA-18 is like wearing a "tailored shirt" as opposed to wearing a loose fitting "Five Brothers Shirt" from Costco!

The radio was tuned to the Merrill Field Tower and permission asked to transition their airspace to the Point MacKenzie side of the Cook Inlet. Upon reaching the Mat-Su side of the Knik Arm, I turned westward and started a descent toward the flats along the Cook Inlet shore. Flying at about five hundred feet above the ground level, I proceeded past the mouth of the Little Susitna River and started flying a grid toward the power lines that fed Anchorage from the Beluga River Power plant, and within a short time, spotted the plane and small pop tent located in a very large swamp. I flew in low and "buzzed" the boys, came on with full power and pulled the nose straight up, hard left rudder, did a wing-over and landed and taxied to their emergency camping location.

Pulling the mixture control to "kill the engine", I opened the window and door of the Super Cub as the propeller came to a stop, and was very warmly greeted by Dan and his friend. It appeared the airplane's engine had "sucked a valve" and stopped running. Dan had sensed the engine trouble but was trying to "nurse" the plane home, and had been keeping a sharp eye out for landing spots. Fortunately for them, the engine chose to "Give Up the Ghost" where it did, or they might have been over timber with no place to land, had they proceeded much farther past this point toward Anchorage. Even worse would have been an emergency landing in the Cook Inlet or in Anchorage proper! He had made a good "Dead Stick" landing (landing with no power) and the airplane was in good condition, other that it was completely "Paralyzed with no Power Plant!"

Dan asked if I would fly his friend to O'Malley Air Strip on my first rescue run, as the friend needed to get to work ASAP! With his gear in the back of my Cub, we made the flight with no problems, and I quickly returned for Dan who had just cut three strong spruce poles to form a tripod for lifting the engine. As we flew toward O'Malley Air Strip, we made "War Plans". He badly needed a good engine to ferry the airplane home.

Fortunately for Dan, in my garage hung the 150 HP Lycoming engine that had powered the PA-18A Super Cub which I had "Totaled" while going after a wolverine in the mountains below Drift River area. I calculated this wolverine had cost me at least $20,000.00, a tremendous amount of stress for me and my family and friends, loss of blood, and a bit of pain! I kept the medical bill down by applying "Butter-fly stitches" to my forehead, instead of following the instruction of the Alaska State Trooper who wanted to take me to the medical clinic for suturing my wounds. A few of my friends shared in the time and effort in salvaging the plane and my gear! That was a Blessing!

When the Drift River crew at their evening dinner table learned of my crash, and the fact I was able to shoot and retrieve the wolverine that I was after, one said, "It was just like a John Wayne Second World War movie! The plane is wrecked, and he crawled out with his gun blazing and shot the wolverine!" When I heard this comparison from their superintendent, I quickly corrected a few things by saying, "I wouldn't make a pimple on John Wayne's fanny", but it was quite a complement being compared to him in this way!"

Before landing at the airstrip I offered my engine for Dan to fly his bird home. He readily accepted and we drove to my home and proceeded to remove any of the Super Cub parts that might interfere with the installation in his Interstate aircraft. He returned with his truck and we placed the engine on a tire and strapped it down. This was delivered to Alaska Air Guides to be flown in a ski equipped Cessna 206, over to the emergency landing site where his plane was tied down. We would fly over early in the morning to remove the old engine and wait for the delivery of my engine around noon.

Up bright and early, within a few minutes of landing near the disabled Interstate aircraft, we had a "Roaring White-Man Fire" and we were working on the removal of the bad engine. My Hunting partner and good friend, Buck had flown over to help in the salvage job! In less than an hour, we had the old engine removed and hanging from the tripod. When the Alaska Air Guides 206 arrived and taxied next to our operation, we removed the good engine and placed the bad engine into his plane and the pilot was off in record time! You have to pay for the "time of operation" of the chartered aircraft, and we tried to make it as quick as possible to keep Dan's bill down!

With the experienced we had gained over the years of working on our airplanes, we soon had the 150 HP engine bolted onto the engine mount, and the prop installed with the safety wire in place on the prop bolts! We did not worry about installing a starter, as the engine was easily started by "hand propping". Before installing the cowling, we test ran the engine in place. She ran as I knew she would!

On our flight back, Dan had no electronics, lights, or radio communication with Merrill Tower, so he followed me, and I informed the tower of our intension. No problem! The following day of landing at O'Malley Air Strip, Dan returned the engine to my garage where we hung it from a cable attached to the heavy steel I-beam that helped support the 28' x 32' building.

Dan delivered his engine to a mutual friend that over-hauled aircraft engines, and was able to install a freshly over-hauled engine in top shape within time to start spring flying. Buck and I were glad to be of help to a fellow airman, and friend.

A Bad Day at Sawmill Bay

The flat bottomed twenty four foot plywood and fiberglass hull of the Kenai Dory with a dog house (small cabin) came skimming into the semi-calm waters of Sawmill Bay. We had made a fast run from Seward, out around Cape Resurrection, into the open waters of the Upper Gulf of Alaska and across Blying Sound to Point Elrington where we again found sheltered waters as we passed South Twin Bay and then North Twin Bay and made a swing to starboard into Elrington Passage. Within a short time we were at the mouth of Sawmill Bay, where the throttle of the Dodge 318, V-8 engine with out-drive was pulled back to just above idle. George and I were to do a little prospecting for red snapper in the area, and we planned to hole up in Saw Mill Bay, using this area as our headquarters for a couple of days. The Kenai Dory came off step and settled deeper into the water, but she still drew very little water. As we slowly turned into the bay, we noticed a strange sight. Standing in a small, silver shiny fourteen foot, very light duty skiff with oars in their locks and blades floating, stood a very weathered old gentleman, if I dare call him such, with his right hand held to his rough, wrinkled, sun browned brow, to shade the bright sunshine, desperately searching the cold blue-green water near the mouth of Saw Mill Bay. As we approached his boat, I recognized that I had met him the year before when I was the skiffman on a purse seine boat out of Valdez and fishing in Prince William Sound. He and his son were drift gillnetting for salmon with their boat and we all had dropped anchor in the same sheltered cove for the night. The father and son team salmon fished in the summer when the season was open, and shrimp potted and halibut long-line fished the other part of the year. I told George that I knew the old gentleman and I hollered over to him as we glided across the water in his direction. "Hello! How's it going?" As we closed the distance between our boats, he replied, "Not too good! I'm looking for my son's body!"

George , an Anchorage Fire Department employee and a good friend of mine from Abbott Loop Chapel where my wife Sharon and I attended church with our three daughters, Laura, Joan, and April, had big ideas of harvesting the "Yellow Eye Rock fish", sometimes falsely called a "Red Snapper" in Alaska.

George had purchased the Kenai Dory with the dog house near the mouth of Ship Creek, at Emards Cannery, in

Anchorage. He had cleaned and sanded and fiberglass coated the hull and beefed the transom and added oak structures where needed, to handle the Dodge 318 cubic inch V-8 engine and the inboard-outboard drive. The factory new engine and out-drive were carefully installed with a little help from a mechanic friend of his. George had previously fished for red snapper in the Gulf of Mexico, when he lived in Texas before his move to Alaska. If we could find a good supply of the yellow eye rockfish, or "red snapper" it is sometimes called up here, we hoped to be able to make enough money to supplement our incomes and hopefully make a living at it.

We were in between jobs where I was working for Clemenson Drilling and I had an opening, giving me time to do this fishing with George. Just before going to Seward, George trailered his boat over to our house so I could do a electrical work on the lights. My neighbor Art Wells was a six-foot-two, red headed Norwegian and asked George, "Where's the oars?" George commented that the boat was too big for paddles or oars. Art reminded George of the paintings he had seen of the Norwegians rowing those huge boats with long oars, and told him, "Well I guess the men were a little more skookum (strong or robust) back then!" As there were no oars, I insisted on bringing my new twenty-five horse power Evinrude outboard as a back-up. George said we were wasting our time bringing it, but if it would keep me happy, put it in. As a precaution, we installed an outboard bracket on the back of his out-drive to enable us to mount the Evinrude if needed, and could steer with the regular controls.

Our first run out of Seward started fine, the blue-green water slapping at the bottom of the dory as we skimmed over the choppy surface. We ran at one power setting for a few minutes, then powered up for awhile and then powered down for a few minutes, trying to break the new engine in as best as we could. She never missed a beat! The swells were longer when we reached the Gulf of Alaska, but the Kenai Dory loped across the big water, and we finally came to the Aialik Cape, where we swung west and north into Aialik Bay, and on into Three Hole Bay where we tried a little fishing with very little success. The Dodge engine had run perfectly up to this point, purring like a kitten. As it was late, we dropped the anchor and spent the night in the sheltered bay, rocked to sleep by the gentle waves. The next morning the temperature was cooler with a little misty rain, and a wind coming out of the south-

southeast. Not to worry. That was until we tried to start the new Dodge 318 engine. The 12 volt battery spun the engine over very fast, but it would not fire. I started checking and we had no spark at the sparkplugs. After much investigation, I decided it was the coil that had gone bad. We needed a part which cost less than ten dollars, and we had no spare! A brand new, very reliable engine and out-drive, and we were shut down far from any help by an inexpensive coil! Murphy has a way of getting into things at times! The old saying goes, "If something can happen, it will happen!"

We looked at each other and then un-wrapped the tarp that covered the Evinrude outboard, and proceeded to mount it on the bracket installed for that purpose. I had brought a six gallon fuel can with premixed gasoline, and a couple of quarts of two cycle outboard oil. With the fuel line attached to the motor, the primer bulb was squeezed until it was tight, and then on the third pull, the Evinrude roared to life, and never missed a beat, except when we later ran out of fuel in the fuel can! Whenever this happened, I had to siphon gasoline from the main fuel tank of the boat by sucking on the end of a rubber hose that had been inserted into the main fuel tank.

Once the fuel filled the hose, I stuck it into the fuel can and it slowly gravity-fed into the six gallon fuel can. Then I mixed the oil in proper proportions. I almost always got a mouth full of gasoline while trying to siphon the gas, all the while being tossed back and forth in the rough seas. I don't usually get seasick, but the gas fumes made me up-chuck my cornflakes! I am thankful God impressed on me to bring the outboard as a backup! After battling all day, we made our way into Resurrection Bay and pulled into Thumb Cove and dropped the pick, and wearily crawled into our sleeping bags and got a little rest. We weighed anchor early the next morning, pointed the bow out into the rough seas, and battled our way into Seward. We then loaded the boat onto the trailer, and made the drive to Anchorage where the engine would be checked and a new coil installed, and with an extra coil packed into the spare parts box. A few days went by, and we returned to Seward, launched the boat again, and made a run for Saw Mill Bay. It was on this run that we spotted the father looking for his son's body! What a sad sight.

When I asked him what had happened, he said his son had been drinking heavily and got "Looped Up on the Kikapoo Joy Juice" and wanted to go to another bay nearby to visit a gal he was sweet-on. He got into a very light and small aluminum skiff with a twenty-five horse power Johnson outboard motor and threw the whip to it. The skiff was so light the bow rode high in the air and when he reached to the mouth of the bay where the wind was whipping the water into whitecaps, a strong gust of wind caught the boat and it launched skyward and flipped over. Looking through the binoculars, the old man viewed his son for the last time!

He sadly told George and me, "I sure need a ride into Whittier to get to a phone and call my wife and tell her what happened. "I don't want the boy's mother to learn about his death on the radio. I don't think she could take it that way." George and I had come out to fish and try to locate an area where we could catch "red snapper" in commercial quantities. We had already been set back by the bad engine coil. George and I looked at each other; I nodded a yes, and likewise did George. Our commercial fishing interest would have to take a back seat today. I almost have to believe God put us there to be of use for Him. God knew that the old gent would need a fast ride into Whittier and that the Kenai Dory with a doghouse would give him a safe ride and arrive in time to notify his wife of their son's death, instead of hearing the bad news on the local radio. George told him, "We'll help you put the skiff away; you can get your gear and climb aboard. We'll give you a ride to Whittier so you can call your wife!" It was a solemn ride to Whittier.

This ended our hunt of 1971 for the Yellow-Eye "Red Snapper" in the Prince William Sound. After taking on more fuel, we made a long run back to Seward, only this time while crossing the upper Gulf of Alaska's Blying Sound, I spent the ride wrapped in rain-gear, shivering in the dark sitting on the bow of the Kenai Dory as she slowly made her way toward Resurrection Cape, me with a flashlight in hand, on the look-out for drift wood and logs that had moved into the area. It was a long cold ride, and one I don't wish to repeat.

At times I wonder why things didn't work out differently for our "red snapper business"? Then, I sometime think George and I may have been placed there and given the opportunity to help someone in need, knowing it was directly opposite to what we wanted to do in the flesh. I must admit I have been helped by others, and I'm sure they had other things to do.

The young man who perished in the accident had been an experienced commercial fisherman, seasoned with harsh weather and rough water, squalls and gales, and with many storms under his belt. But the "Fickle Finger of Fate" waited for him as he made his last "Run To Romance"! The thought of "Channel Number Five" had been too much for him!

TERRORIST ALERT AT THE JUNEAU, ALASKA, AIRPORT!

It was 2008 and I was busy drilling water wells in Seward, Alaska, when receiving a phone call from my "Hunting Partner" and owner of "Statewide Blasting and Perforating Service", Buck. It appeared the Pelican Job was almost ready for us to show up with our "Dynamite and Blasting Caps and Powder Punch"! In Pelican the narrow trail leading up to a new water storage tank needed to be widened, and they had encountered bedrock that could not be excavated. It would have to be drilled and loaded with explosives, and blasted to loosen the formation in able to excavate it.

I worked "over-time" to get the well completed that I was working on, and was driven by my wife to the Kenai Airport for my flight into Anchorage, where I met Buck for our flight to Juneau. And as the weather in Juneau does not always cooperate, fog made it impossible to land there, so we were dropped off at Sitka, to await a later flight into Juneau. The weather reports did not look good for the evening flight into Juneau, so we thought of another option! We knew we would have to fly from Juneau by floatplane into Pelican, so why not just fly floatplane from Sitka to

Pelican and avoid the Juneau airport altogether!

After checking air charter operations, we located Harris Air, and made arrangements for the flight, moved our gear to their location and waited for the time of departure. It was an uneventful flight to Pelican, thank goodness! I have had enough "White-Knuckle Flights" to last a lifetime already! And on many of the flights, I was "Pilot In Command"!

With our gear unloaded onto the water soaked wharf, we made our way on the wooden walkway that comprised the "raised sidewalk" of Pelican. Most of the buildings were supported by the tall creosote treated "Piling Post", similar to telephone poles. If you dropped a quarter or half-dollar piece onto the sidewalk, it probably would fall through the "cracks between the planks" and down at least twenty feet or more into the clear, blue ocean water! We were shown to our rooms with large beds and a television sitting on a table. Over on the floor rested an old cardboard box containing a few old video tapes along with a small collection of "Dog-Eared" Louis L'Amour paperback books with well worn covers. Across from the bedrooms was a kitchen-dining area with refrigerator and a four burner cook stove. Most of the skillets and cooking pans were the "Teflon Coated", and had long past lived their usefulness, as the coating was scratched and pealing on almost all of them. They would have to do!

The Superintendent, Mike, did the drilling of the holes after we located and marked the spot to place the charges of explosives. After the holes were drilled, we measured the depths, and decided what "Delay Blasting Cap" to use in each hole. I made up most of the charges, and after using a brass "Powder Punch" to punch a hole into the "Nitroglycerin base Dynamite", I inserted the electric Blasting Cap into the hole, and took two "half-hitches around the stick" with the wire and eased the explosive to the bottom of the hole. We then placed any needed sticks of dynamite into the hole and onto the original charge. After the charge was in place, we "stemmed" the rest of the hole with small "pea gravel" to hold the explosion in the lower portion of the hole, and fracture the rock formation. One occasion, the hole in the bedrock looked as if it were blocked by a piece of shale rock, I casually reached for the Mini-Mag flashlight that was carried on my belt, and shown the light into the hole. Fortunately the hole was clear, I replaced the light to its holster and did not think about it again, until a few days later at the airport, when confronted by the Security Officer.

After working a few days, we completed our explosive work and were to fly to Juneau the following day for our return flight to Anchorage and home. As was customary, we laundered our coveralls and clothing that had come into contact with the Nitroglycerin dynamite. Gloves were then placed into air-tight "Zip Lock Bags" and then into our duffel bags. We kept our rain gear unpacked, as we would need it while going to the floatplane and when walking in Juneau. The pilot made a smooth landing on the water and we were soon delivered to the Juneau airport, to check in for our Alaska Airlines flight into Anchorage.

Buck and I have been checked by the Airport Security enough times that we had placed our pocket knives and belt knives and any "sharp tool" into our checked luggage. I removed my keys, coins, and any other item in my pockets, and then placed them with my small "Mini-Mag Flashlight" into the tray to be inspected. I guessed the Security Personal were relatively new to the job, as they seemed a bit nervous. I waited before going through the "Security Screen" while the Guard did a little "Wipe and Analyze" of my "Mini-Mag Flashlight".

All of a sudden I saw the Guard's eyebrows raised to "Attention"! He looked toward me, pointed his finger straight at me and said, "Now Don't You

Move!" I responded by asking him, "Did you locate some Goodie on my flashlight?" I said, "I'm not too surprised, as I was punching Nitroglycerine dynamite on a job in Pelican yesterday, and forgot to wash the flashlight." He called for his Supervisor, who came over from his desk to this location, and glanced over at me. I did not know this gentleman by name, but had seen him over the years while traveling Alaska. He said, "Don't worry about that guy he's been around for a Long Time!" I was released and was able to make the flight towards home! In Anchorage, I boarded a small commuter airplane, and the "Security" was not as rigid!

Sometimes it pays to keep you're "Reputation Clean"! My Father used to say, "Use your head for something besides a "Knot to keep your spinal cord from unraveling!" He was right! I have been doing explosives work since the 1970's and still have my hands and all of my fingers! The only thing that has been damaged is my hearing from the loud drilling machines I've run! Years ago, we didn't have the good hearing protection we do now!

If you want to be an airline pilot or have a Commercial Drivers License, don't drink and drive and get too many DUI tickets!

Try not to do anything that will hinder your opportunities later in life.

Don't Drink and Drive, and possibly lose your driver's license, or worse, cause injury or death to some innocent person.

Don't be "STUPID" and use drugs! I have friends and relatives that have lost children to drug use! It is a Waste!

"Common Sense" is not very common anymore!

THE TWENTY THOUSAND DOLLAR WOLVERINE!

The sun peeked over the eastern ridge and caught me loading my truck in preparation of another day's flying. Just three days before, I had met my hunting buddies Chuck and Jimmy at Tustumena Lake for a good rabbit hunt. We had landed on the frozen lake, taxied our planes near the shore, and combed the area for the critters. Afterwards, I helped Chuck drop his plane off at Northern Lights Avionics for radio work. With his radios in good repair, he was ready to take advantage of the extremely low tides for clam digging and invited me to go with him. Chuck was flying with his thirty inch Air Streak Tundra Tires, and 93 Charlie was performing exceptionally well!

My PA-18 Super Cub was still mounted on the Snyder 4000 fixed penetration wheel-skis, but I knew they would work fine on the wet sand of the exposed low tide-flat as it would be fairly smooth. There was too much snow left in the out-country for me to remove the skis at that time. I had many snow landings to do before removing them and installing my large Tundra Tires.

It was a clear and crisp morning when Chuck and I met at the O'Malley Airstrip, checked oil-levels, polished windshields, and topped off the fuel tanks located in the wings of the Super Cubs, drained fuel sumps, primed engines and fired off the engines to warm. The wing covers had been used over-night to keep the frost from adhering to the upper wing's surface and they had been removed and thrown into the truck to dry before replacing them into the nylon bag that protected them while being stored. We each gave the other a "Thumbs Up" signal as we climbed into our planes.

I was carrying two five gallon metal cans of gasoline and a galvanized tractor-funnel with chamois-cloth gas filter for my plane as I wanted to do a little scouting around after the clam digging. We were going after the six inch and larger "Razor Clams" from the Polly Creek and another area. They were so good that I could eat a large mounded plate-full of these clams after they were dissected and cleaned, dipped into egg batter and cracker-crumbs, and fried to a light golden brown! They were gooooooood! I have often had friends ask how I could eat so much and not get as fat as a hog? Well, at that point in time, I was working, or trapping, or hunting or doing something to burn every bit of excess fat! If I'd been performing like a "Couch-Potato" as they were, I would have been as obese as they were. Or Fatter!

We obtained permission to cross the air-space of Merrill Airfield airspace and the Anchorage International Airport airspace. We reached the Pt. MacKenzie side and switched radio frequencies and as usual had a good visit talking back and forth as we flew and looked, and checked the area as we traveled toward the Big Susitna River.

The air was very smooth and we had no trace of turbulence near Mount Susitna, a rare day to say the least! Much of the snow had melted in the low-lying country near the beach, but up on the side hills, winters snow still held the landscape. As is my custom, being a hunter and trapper, I drifted over to the low foothills in search of animal tracks, where I saw an occasional fox or marten track. There were also a few tracks made by wolves, but they looked old and not worth following.

We flew past the Beluga and Tyonek areas, and past the Chakachatna and McAuthur Rivers and across the Redoubt Bay State Critical Habitat Area and past Drift River, but as I passed Cannery Creek, I noticed wolverine tracks. I pointed the nose of the Super Cub downward and saw they were "fresh tracks" and seeing the heel of the track knew the wolverine was traveling the same direction I was headed. Oh how I wish I had just

"Tipped my hat and bid him Adieu". Instead my "Hunting Blood" was aroused, and I radioed Chuck that I had spotted wolverine tracks and was following them.

This was rough, mountainous terrain, in which wolverine are usually found, and he had been hunting ptarmigan as he checked each alder thicket that was exposed. The snow was very deep and most of the alder and willow bushes and trees were completely covered. There were no leaves exposed or grass or blowing snow to indicate a wind condition as I flew along following my quarry.

As I crossed a deep valley, I saw the tracks climbing upward to the top of a long flat ridge on the mountain's top, and sitting at one end of the hog-back was the beautiful wolverine. I made a pass along the side of the hog-back and calculated it to be a landing area long enough and looked to be twelve to fifteen feet wide, enough for me to touch-down and stop. As I came on with full flaps and made the set-up for landing, the wolverine spotted the airplane and bailed off the end of the ridge, going all the way to the valley floor.

This again was not your usual landing spot as it was a "One-Way Canyon" and would have to be approached from the Inlet side. A cow moose lay in the deep snow near the creek that drained the valley, but I could see that I had enough room to touch down with the skis and stop before reaching the moose. I flew straight away from the landing area, pulled the airplane up steeply, hit the rudder and did a "Wing-Over", on with power and caught the plane before it fell much distance at all, and came in for the landing "Hanging On the Prop". As soon as the skis touched the snow, I "dumped the flaps" and opened the side window, kicked the rudder to the left and climbed out of the Cub. I grabbed the stock of the Armalite AR-180 that I had named "The Black Ugly", un-folded it into position, flipped the scope covers off and threw it to my shoulder. The wolverine was just running at the base of a long ridge to get behind a large hump, and I squeezed-off a round of the full metal jacketed bullet as he dipped behind the hump. He was gone. I hastily removed my snowshoes from the wing-strut and placed them onto my white Army surplus "Vapor Boot" and made a "Bee-Line" to the hump where the wolverine was last seen, and when getting there, noticed a few hairs that had been cut by the bullet, but no sign of blood, indicating a missed shot at the wolverine. I looked in back of the hump and saw where the wolverine had traveled and entered an alder patch that extended high on another ridge that overlooked the valley. By this time, my adrenalin was starting to "perk", and I snow-shoed up the steep slope as fast as I could, huffing and puffing as I went. When I reached to top of the slope and looked downward into the alder limbs, I spotted the wolverine's tracks and followed them with the rifle scope. The wolverine traveled across the edge of the ridge, then dropped down into the valley. I watched as he traveled across the valley floor, too far away to get a shot at him with this rifle. Had I been using my long range .244 Remington instead, I might have had a chance at him at that distance, but not with the "Black Ugly"!

Being somewhat endowed with "ingenuity", I removed my snowshoes and used them as a sled by sitting on them and sliding down the steep slope toward the Super Cub. When I reached the bottom, I re-installed the snowshoes and quickly made my way to the plane. I thought to myself, "If I get another shot at him, I'll throw everything I have at him!" With this thought in mind, I inserted a thirty round clip into the rifle and a thirty round clip in my front right pants-pocket.

Chuck was now flying overhead and tracked the wolverine as he crossed the valley, up the steep mountain-side and onto a fairly level area high-up on the mountainside. "You'd better get with it if you are going to get another shot at him!" Chuck called out on the radio. "If he makes it to the next ravine, he'll be gone!" "I'm on my way!" was my reply as I hit the plane's starter, closed the lower door and window and threw the whip to the one hundred and fifty horses under the hood of the Cub! I made a high-speed turn and pointed the nose of the airplane toward the Inlet, pulled full flaps, back on the stick and I was climbing like a "home-sick Angel".

I made a climbing turn as I approached the mountainside where Chuck had last seen the wolverine. When reaching the area I made a fast assessment of the situation. There was a relatively flat area at the base of the main slope of the mountain and there is where I quickly decided to land. I pulled full flaps and started a descending right turn, but realized I was too high to get into that spot and came on with power and flew toward the Inlet crossing a three tiered steep gulley and past a long sloping hog-back ridge that was level on top, and the gulley fell-away as it drained toward the north, in the direction the wolverine was headed.

As I flew on the outside of this hog-back ridge I saw that the middle portion of the three tiered gully should be long enough to safely land

the little Super Cub. There were no
leaves or trees sticking up from the
snow to give an indication of a wind
or in what direction the wind might be
blowing. I had pulled full flaps, ran
the trim control forward and started
making a left turn to set-up for an
up-hill landing on the middle tier of
the gully. My eyes kept flashing from
the landing area back to the wolverine
that was to my right at the base of
the main mountain. What I did not
realize was there was a wind blowing
from the Inlet and as it passed over
the hog-back, it formed a down-draft.
I was making a slow left turn when all
of a sudden I felt the Cub shudder
violently and jabbed the throttle
forward, but too late to catch the
airplane and she started a stall. The
left wing dropped and I was headed for
the snow-covered ground, nose first.
I had no time for a long prayer, but
just called out, "God, don't let me
get hurt too bad!"

I didn't have enough room under
me to recover from the stall before
hitting the ground! This was an "Oh
S--t" of the highest degree! I almost
break-out into a sweat as I write this
now! It may sound stupid, but I
wasn't afraid of of being killed, what
bothered me was the thought of being
crippled and not be able to provide
for my family. I have often asked
myself, "Why did I not take up the

occupation of selling shoes, or selling Tupper-Ware or working at the hardware store or some other safe job rather than the adventuresome occupations or hobbies I had followed! I had longed for adventure as a teenager before leaving Memphis, Tennessee, and traveling to Alaska, and I have been given a huge-helping of it!

I was looking straight down at the snow when the airplane's left wing-tip and nose hit the ground about the same time, the left wing bent and the plane's belly tubes buckled allowing the floor-board to come up within an inch of my legs. As we hit, I was thrown forward and my forehead struck my whisky-compass, breaking the glass and allowing the fluid to run out. My right knee went forward hard enough to hit the lower dash and cut the skin open. I hadn't realized my forehead was split open until I felt the burning sensation of the gasoline that trickled onto my forehead as one of the five gallon cans in the baggage compartment started to leak. I rubbed my hand across my forehead and it was immediately covered with blood. "Lord, I've got to get out of here before she catches on fire!" I said and pulled the quick-release lever on my Crop-Duster Safety Seat-belt and dropped forward, as the plane was standing on its nose, with the tail pointed high into the air. I then tried to push the right window and door open, but it was jammed, as the landing gear had collapsed and the right landing gear and wheel-skis were folded up against the side of the plane and blocking the door, thinking for about a second or two about the situation I was in and what to do, and with my right elbow, drew back and hit the window as hard as I could with my elbow, and busted the plexiglas window out! I somehow climbed out the window and was rudely brought to a stop when the long thirty round ammo clip in my front pocket hung-up on the window frame! "Dang!" I placed my feet against the "X Brace" in the "sky-light of the plane and pushed as hard as I could with my legs, and felt the heavy Alaska Sleeping-Bag Company wool pant pocket rip, allowing me to drop onto the snow and get away from the plane before it caught on fire. I could see smoke coming from the engine cowling and I said, "Lord, don't let her burn!" as we had just recently cancelled the insurance on the plane! I quickly thought and reached into the airplane, grabbed my coat and my rifle case and walked away from the plane, in case she exploded into flames. That did not happen. She did not burn!

I heard an airplane overhead, and then saw the belly and Air Streak tires of Chuck's plane as he flew over-head, low and slow. I waved my hand to him to indicate I was all right, and wiped the blood from my right eye allowing me to see more clearly. "Praise the Lord, I'm not hurt too bad, I might as well get that wolverine. I've paid a Heck of a Price to do that!" I reached for my gun case, and removed the rifle to find the hinged stock had been broken at the pistol-grip area where the stock hinges to make it a "Folding Stock".

I looked to the base of the main mountain to see where the wolverine might have gone, and too my amazement the wolverine was standing and holding a ptarmigan in its mouth. Well, I guess it was about the way I am. I usually eat "popcorn" when viewing an exciting movie. Instead of popcorn, the wolverine had caught himself a ptarmigan to munch on! I walked to the other side of the airplane and tried to get a good sitting position in which to shoot, nothing doing!

The stock was about as stiff as a "wet-noodle" and no way could I get a good "bead" on the wolverine. Not wanting to give-up on the idea of shooting the wolverine, I just lay down on my belly, poked the pistol grip down into the snow to steady the rifle, and turned the scope to seven power took a good aim and squeezed the trigger, "Blam! Blam!" I had a wolverine to skin!

Unknown to me, when I crashed my Super Cub, I must have squeezed the microphone trigger on the control stick, as all Chuck heard was a "Ugggggh" as the air was knocked from me! My ear-phones were knocked off and I could not hear Chuck calling, "Vern! Vern!" and he thought I had been Killed! He told me later that he was crying as he called out to me, as he thought I was Dead! Now let me tell you something. We're not talking about a "Wimp"! Chuck was as tough as a "Boiled Owl"! If he had any fat on him, it would have to be beef fat on his chin from a steak he had just eaten! He could dang-near "Whip His Weight in Wolverines!" Stronger than a Bull! Chuck switched frequencies to the Kenai Airport Tower and informed them there had been an airplane crash, and he thought it was a fatal! The boys at the tower got on the job pronto, and called the State Troopers, gave them the message, and Kenai Air was notified they needed a helicopter ride to the crash site.

"Meanwhile back at the Ranch!" I knew we would have to fly and land a Super Cub in this gully to salvage the plane, so I decided to walk up the slope and stamp-out a marker for landing, which I did. After many years of skinning fur and game animals

I thought, no need for that wolverine to cool down and get stiff, so I snowshoed over and picked him up, still holding the ptarmigan in this mouth! I reached into my pocket and removed my "Muskrat Skinner" knife I used for fine work, and proceeded to the job at hand. And as I have skinned many wolverines in my career of trapping, I soon had the hide "cased" from his butt to his head and was about to cut the flesh at his nose, when I heard the "Whop! Whop! Whop!" of the helicopter as they homed-in on my ELT that was transmitting a distress call! My ELT was activated when I crashed the plane, and automatically started sending a distress signal that indicated my location.

As the State Trooper stepped out of the chopper, I stuffed the wolverine hide into the rifle case with the "Black Ugly", and handed it to the Trooper to place in the chopper, "You can't haul that thing in here!" the chopper pilot exclaimed! (You are not supposed to haul game animals or their parts in a chopper in Alaska. The Trooper said, "Let him haul the thing home, he's paid a hell of a price for it already!" The Pilot said no more.

The Trooper had me switch off the ELT (Emergency Locator Transmitter) and said we need to get the radios out of the plane if we could. He said the

215

"Pickers" will be here when they hear of the crash. I could not remove the King Radios as the Allen-wrench that I normally used to install or remove the radios had been knocked from its location and could not be seen. I grabbed the gas cans and set them outside of the plane, to keep more gasoline from dripping into the airplane. After we had done as much as we could, we climbed into the still idling helicopter. As I strapped my safety belt, the Trooper said, "We'll get you to the medical clinic and they will suture you up." I told him that won't be necessary, just get me to a mirror and a few band-aids and I'll take care of it myself! He insisted on getting to the medical clinic, so no need of arguing with him, but I was not going to run up a medical bill as I had already blew all of our savings, crashing the airplane!

When we arrived at the Kenai Helicopter hanger, I went in to the bathroom and opened their "First Aid Kit". Had I been an OSHA Inspector, they would have flunked the test. The only things in the First Aid Cabinet were a bottle of aspirin, eye wash liquid in a bottle, an odd shaped gauze-bandage, a few Q-tips, extra roll of toilet-paper and two women's "Sanitary Napkins"! Not even any iodine! When Chuck arrived I asked if I could use his First Aid Kit, as we always carried a well equipped kit, and he went to his plane and delivered it to me. I used betadine to clean the long cuts in my forehead and using my knife, cut notches in the Band-aids to form "Butterfly Stitches", applied it to one side of the cut, and then pulled the cut together, and applied the other side. By evening, my forehead had swollen so much my forehead looked like the bill on a baseball hat! Had the swelling gone inward, it probably would have killed me! I must say the "Butter-fly Stitches" were the way to go, as there is no sign of a scare on my forehead, they were quick and painless to apply, and I didn't receive a medical bill for applying them! If you are going to ride with me, you better be ready for some "in-the-field-type repairs because we're not running up a huge medical bill if I can sew you up!" I actually carry a suturing needle in my wallet most of the time.

Before Chuck arrived, a mechanic came from the hanger and asked what shape the airplane was in? I told him it was totaled, but had lots of good parts left. He then said, "Well, it won't be long before the "Pickers" get there!" indicating the "Lowly Father-Less Men" that steal parts from a plane crash or wreck without notifying and getting permission to do so from the owner. I told him, "Well, I

217

might have wrecked the airplane and broke my rifle stock, but I still shot the wolverine. Tell those XXXXXX----s if they come over to get my plane, I'll be waiting for them!" And I meant it! I would have shot them like rabid dogs if they had tried that with me! The Trooper saw that I was as "Hot as a Foxes Rear in a Pepper Patch" as my Dad used to say, and told the folks at Kenai Helicopter to "Do Not Divulge the Location of the Wreck"!

I called my hunting partner Buck, and as he did not answer the phone, told him I was in Kenai and would call him when I got to town. By the message, he knew something was wrong. Fortunately, my wife Sharon was not home when Chuck and I drove by to use the phone to call Buck. I informed Buck of the accident and the need to fly down there on skis to start the salvage operation as soon as possible. Before leaving the house, I placed a note near the front door telling Sharon. "I had a little problem with the plane, I'm okay. Will see you tonight. Love, Vern". With this placed where she could see when she arrived at home, we drove to the airport, and hopped into Chuck's plane and flew to Birchwood Airport, where Buck was removing his Tundra Tires in preparation of installing his Aero 3000 Skis.

My good friend Jimmy had been notified as he came to the airport to help in the salvage operation. The National Transportation Safety Board had sent a message to a Birchwood aircraft shop, wanting to talk to me. Jimmy relayed the message and I gave the fellow a call. The NTSB wanted to know what had happened, had the engine stopped or any other failure of the aircraft. I told him No, the aircraft had not failed me, I had screwed-up! In that case you may salvage the aircraft! Otherwise, they would have taken the plane to do research as to why the plane stalled! Many times when a pilot "screws-up" they say they had carburetor-ice, or the engine quit or some other excuse instead of coming-out and admitting they "SCREWED-UP". I was told a few years later, "It takes a lot of Ada-Boys to make up for one OH S--T!" And they are right! I would have to dig deep into the back-pocket (wallet) to pay for this one!

When I told the NTSB representative that the fault of the crash lay on me instead of the airplane, their investigation was over! He then released the aircraft to me. Up until that time the plane had become the property of the NTSB until an investigation of the cause of the crash was completed. He called Kenai Helicopters and ordered then to with-hold the location of the crash, to give me an opportunity to salvage the plane before the "Pickers" could get to it!

We now had the skis on Buck's Super Cub and were ready for the sad flight to "Vern's Notch" as the area was named. When we reached the general area, we all landed on a frozen lake and had a "Powwow". Buck and I would fly to the crash site; remove the "Tail-Feathers", radios, wheel-skis and any other thing Buck could fly in his Cub to the frozen lake we had landed on. Jimmy and Chuck would fly the parts to town while I again rode in the backseat of Buck's plane. Before departing, Buck handed me his camera as I was going to video the crash site, airplane and its damage and so-on. I am glad I had stomped out a landing spot, as it made the landing much easier and safer. We landed up-hill, then turned around and taxied down to 8081 Charlie, who was still standing on its nose. It was a sad site indeed! I stayed bent-over most of the afternoon, using wrenches and sockets removing the parts. With the blood forced to my head when bend over, my forehead swelled even farther out! Now, it was a Heck of a site! I could have done a Great "Aspirin or Head-ache advertisement for television"!

While we worked on the airplane, Jimmy flew to the Drift River Oil Production Facility and asked if the helicopter at their facility could be chartered to fly my airplane to their runway to be later flown into Anchorage. When Jimmy was talking on the phone, the supervisor and crew were gathered round to hear what was going on. There have been many airplane crashes when hunters have wrecked their birds while pursuing the fur and game animals in the area. As Jimmy talked to the Anchorage office, they were telling of the many salvage jobs they had done in the past and had been cheated out of the payment by the plane's owner. Jimmy spoke up and said, "This is Vern Nowell, and he has been in Alaska many years and owns his own water drilling business. He'll pay his bill!" When the Drift River supervisor heard my name, he piped-up and said "I know Vern. He's a friend of mine! Let me have that phone!" Ron told the Anchorage office that I would pay any bill I ran up and he would personally vouch for me! With the thought of using the Drift River helicopter for the salvage job, Jimmy flew back to the lake, and Buck later flew him up to the crash site to help with the work.

Before long, we heard the "Whop! Whop! Whop!" of the rudders as the helicopter flew to the site, gently hovered near the wreck and landed. Ron got out of the plane and said, "This flight is on me! I wanted to see what she looks like now!" Back at the Drift River Camp, the crew was almost as excited as they would be at a movie when the action is at its peak! Ron said, "The crew is talking about the plane crash and Vern climbing out with his rifle blazing and killing the wolverine, just like a John Wayne Movie when he gets shot down by the Japanese! There have been a lot of plane crashes in the area, but no one but Vern has ever got the animal after a crash!" I told Ron, "I wouldn't make a Pimple on John Wayne's fanny, but it was nice being compared to him!"

The following day, the chopper from Drift River flew to the site and tried to raise the crippled Cub, but did not have enough "Lift" to accomplish the task. When I received the invoice for the "No-Go Try to Lift", helicopter invoice, my wife made out a check and mailed it to them. They had made a try at it, and I paid for their time.

I called Kenai Air and talked to Tim Miller, Chief Pilot, asked if they thought they would be able to ferry the Cub to Kenai. He thought they could make the lift with no problems as they were using very light landing gear as opposed to the heavy pontoons that were on the Drift River Chopper.

We had removed the engine after the first chopper's "No-Go" attempt, and Eskimo Floyd flew his J-3 Cub with ninety horse engine down to haul the my plane's engine to Birchwood for me. I had driven to Birchwood with my Ford F-250 Crew-Cab loaded with a full one hundred and thirty gallon gasoline tank with a twelve volt transfer pump, to fuel the Boy's birds that were helping in the salvage operation. Over the years, I have been able to help others when they need it, and I very much appreciated all the help my friends were giving me. No questions asked or implied! We tied the O-320 engine to keep it from moving forward and backwards in the back seat of Floyd's plane. Floyd was videoed as the engine was loaded and as he taxied to a parking spot to be out of the way of the chopper. I told Buck later, "We've taken more video footage on this salvage job than they would have if there had been a Presidential Shooting!"

We finally heard the Kenai Air helicopter 'Whopping" our way. He landed and again I signed a "Release Paper" giving them permission to "Drop" the load if their safety required it! I will say this, "That boy knew what he was doing! There was no playing around with him as he powered-up enough to take the slack out of the cable, tested the weight of the load, and then was off and running toward the Inlet. I learned later, he landed on the beach and tied a fifteen foot long spruce tree to the tail to make the load fly correctly!

Not long after the chopper flew the fuselage and wings, Floyd got his ski-mounted Piper J-3 in the air, We gathered up our gear, and spiffed up the area and Jimmy took the head of the wolverine that still held the ptarmigan's head, and later mounted it on his fire-place mantel!

The following day, Chuck and I drove my F-250 Crew Cab with our Goose-neck, four-horse Hale Trailer to Kenai and loaded 8081 Charlie for the ride back home. I went into the office and wrote a check for the salvage work they had provided.

My wife Sharon had been my nurse during all of this, cleaning the wound on my forehead, and taking care of me. I remember the first time she cleaned the wound, crying and had a hard time with it. We had got the plane home, and after a good supper that consisted of Moose-meat Swiss-steak, gravy, potatoes, frozen yellow corn and a dessert, I made the statement, "Yes, that was a Twenty-thousand dollar wolverine!" Our youngest daughter April, who stood on a stool at the kitchen sink while washing dishes, turned and exclaimed, "Dad, a Twenty Thousand Dollar Wolverine! Let's go and get some more!" My wife Sharon then interjected the truth of the mater into the conversation. "April, your Dad did not mean he could sell the wolverine for Twenty Thousand Dollars. He meant the Wolverine Cost him Twenty Thousand Dollars!" And I must add, "A lot of work, sweat, and blood!"

When I talked to the NTSB and informed the wreck was my fault, I think they might have notified the Federal Aviation Administration of the accident as I received a phone call from one of FAA's "Flight Inspectors" who after finding out that I was "Hunting" when I had the accident, proceeded to "Rake me over the hot-coals!" He demanded that I come in immediately for a "Check Ride". I informed him, I would take a check ride whenever I was able to get a Super Cub to take the "Check Ride" in, as I did not fly Cessna 152's! He later called me and even told me if I did not take a check ride now, to bring in my Pilots License and surrender it to him! This caused my bladder to feel Extremely Full! I told him, that I had a friend with a Super Cub that I could use for the flight but it had Air Streak Tundra Tires on it and I had heard the FAA didn't think too highly of them! (At

225

the time, the very good, and becoming very popular tire was not approved by the FAA. They felt the tires gave the pilot a "False Sense of Security" and they were lured into taking chances they might not take if they were not using the Tundra Tire). HE BLEW HIS STACK! I knew if I took my check ride with that fellow, there might be trouble involved, and probably on the pavement before we got into the plane! I had a hard time dealing with his "Superior Attitude". I do not believe he was an "Alaskan" at that time.

Well, as we had flying to do in Southeastern Alaska in the spring, I was looking as hard as I could to find a replacement Super Cub. I finally found a Cub owned by Rick Schneider who had developed and patented a good "Fixed-Penetration Wheel Ski". I purchased this Super Cub, 4302 Zulu on April 23, 1983.

May 5, 1983, I called the FAA and asked to speak to the "Flight Inspector" that had been hounding me for the check-ride. He had gone to Kenai and would not be back until the following week. I told her, he has been after me for weeks to get a check ride. I had just purchased another Super Cub and wanted a Check-Ride tomorrow. She handed me off to another "Flight Inspector" and he told me what time to come in. The following morning I introduced myself to Ed Bettinger and we sat down at his desk and talked for awhile. It appeared we had mutual friends over the years, and we got along real well. Before we stepped outside, he said, "Vern, right now you have one-hundred per cent. When you start making mistakes, that's when I start deducting from you! Go out and do a Pre-Flight, as I have something to do."

I walked out to the plane and did as thorough a "Pre-Flight as one might have done before heading out over the Atlantic Ocean!" I even "Finger Tested" the fuel tanks, as was my habit anyway. I did not see him watching, but as soon as I completed the task, he walked onto the tarmac and told me what he had in mind. We both got into the Cub, and I had installed a "Rear-Stick" which enabled him to steer and fly the airplane from the back-seat. I received clearance from the Ground Control and taxied out toward the runway, did a "Run-Up" and then switched to "Tower Control". After being given a clearance I rolled onto the runway and pushed the throttle forward, and we were off.

Once we cleared International Airport's airspace, we changed frequencies and switched the radio to the "Intercom Mode" where we could talk to each other without transmitting over the airwaves. He had me do forty-five mile per hour "Slow Flight, Full Flap" turns and that type of flying. After a few of those, he said, "Vern, give me the airplane, close your eyes and I'm going to take over. When I tell you, I want you to take control, and maintain level flight." With this command, I released my hold on the control stick and let him have the airplane. He pulled back on the stick where the plane was almost straight up and ready to enter a stall and spin. When given the command, I opened my eyes, took control, came on with power and never lost any altitude. After about three or four of those maneuvers, he said, "Let's fly to Merrill Field and do a few "Touch-and-Go" landings.

I contacted Merrill Field and was given permission to enter the pattern, and as we were coming in for a landing, I greased the plane onto the runway and started to apply power for the "Go-Around" when he said, "No need for a Go-around. Take me to the Piper Center and let me off!" When he climbed from the plane he stated, "Vern, you don't have any problems. Just be a little more careful when you're out hunting again!" With that remark, he bid me "Good Bye". Ed Bettinger was an old time Alaskan Pilot and he knew his business! I wish there were more of his kind out there!

"THE PICKERS"

If you have never learned about the "Pickers", the "Low-Life Scum" let me tell you a disgusting true tale! This short but true story should give you an idea what the "Pickers" are really like and just how "Honorable" they are!

One Sunday morning my wife and girls and I were just getting ready to leave the house for church. I received a phone call from my hunting partner Buck who said, "I need some help. Brian was killed yesterday in a plane crash!" I told my wife Sharon to take the girls and go to church, and just pray for Brian's wife and little boy, and also pray everything goes okay with Buck and me as we try to salvage the airplane. I went and changed clothes and drove to our Super Cub about a block away at O'Malley Airstrip. I flew to Birchwood Airstrip, and as was my custom landed in the gravel "Thresh-hold of the runway" to protect my Tundra Tires from being "scuffed" by the asphalt surface of the main-runway. As I reached the pavement, I turned and taxied over to where Buck was waiting. We had a "customary hug" and then climbed into our Cubs and flipped the radio on and transmitted our intentions, taxed out onto the runway and fire-walled the birds! There is nothing like flying a good PA-18 Super Cub. A PA-12 is a good plane, but they always feel like a "Five Brothers Shirt" to me. They fit too loose for me to be real comfortable in them! Now you take a good PA-18 and it's like putting on a custom-fitted Pendleton shirt! The trim on my Cub was adjusted so finely, if the wind was calm, I could lean hard to one side of the cockpit and the airplane would gently turn that direction! I could fly with a coffee cup on the dash by the tubes and fly with my feet off the pedals, the trim adjusted, hold elevation and straight ahead. It was nice!

It seemed Brian and a friend were flying from the west side of Cook Inlet and were following and inspecting a small creek that sometimes contains king salmon. Unbeknown to Brian, there was a stiff wind coming out of Turnagain Arm. As he slowly flew the Cub at full flaps and banked steeply to see if there were any kings in the hole that was formed by a bend in the creek, he made a steep "Down-wind" turn and the wind hit him on the tail, dropping his airspeed and causing the wing to stall and the airplane to go into the "Moose-Hunter's Stall". This is where the plane inverts and comes straight down nose first, with no time or room to recover at the elevation they were flying. This happened just across from Birchwood Airport on the Knik Side. As Brian did not have his shoulder harness on, he was thrown forward and busted his head on the dash and tubes. The rear passenger was thrown forward into the metal frame of Brian's front-seat, and received head and brain injuries. A rescue mission was launched as soon as the accident was discovered and the passenger and Brian's body removed from the wreckage. This had happened on Saturday evening.

Sunday morning was bright and clear as Buck and I flew high across the silt laden waters and dropped low to view the wrecked airplane that was still standing on its nose. We landed on the silt-sand tide-flat area and taxied up as close as we could get. The scene was disgusting! As we neared the crash-site we saw that someone had removed Brian's thirty-inch Air Streak Tundra Tires and stole them! We got out of our planes and walked over to the sad scene. You could see the foot-prints they had made while removing the wheel and tires, all the time standing in the large pool of blood. The ground was still painted a crimson color! What "Low-Life Boil-Sucker" could be so dastardly as to steal like that? The plane now could only be sold at a fraction of its value as compared to

when it was in fly-condition. The Air
Streak Tundra Tires mounted on the
Cleveland wheel with brakes were very
expensive and could have been sold to
help Brian's wife and little boy. The
family would need as much money to
help them survive after losing the
father and husband that had provided
for them as he mounted the game
animals in his Taxidermy Shop.

Brian was gone. And "Chalk up another
one for the Pickers!"

I often wonder if they ever washed the
blood off the soles of their boots?

ILLEGAL "SHARE-CROPPING IN ALASKA"

I'm looking at the Webster's New World Dictionary, at the word "share-crop: to work (land) for a share of the crop, as a tenant farmer." Well I have been involved in a "share-crop" venture, all the while unbeknownst to me, and was cheated out of my share, and me being the land-owner! This was a very "low-down" trick to have played on oneself! Hopefully this never happens to you!

I believe the year was 2008 and it was the month of April. My good friend Cole, who is a top-notch construction contractor, home builder, honest as the Alaska mid-summer's day is long, straight as an arrow, good father and husband, and avid sportsman was thinking of purchasing property in the Mat-Su valley to build a cabin for his family to enjoy, away from the sometimes damp and wet Seward weather where they reside. He knew my wife and I had property up near Willow, Alaska, and Cole wanted to look at it, with thoughts of purchasing it from me. I had not been to the property for at least four or five years and I wanted to check on the little cabin I had started building on it.

We decided on a day in which to drive up, me driving from Nikiski and Cole and a friend, Tim, driving up from Seward. They planned on bringing their

Honda 4-wheelers for transportation, but I advised against it. The snow in Seward is sometimes very damp and heavy and packs down to offer a firm surface to operate the 4-wheelers on. On the other hand, the snow conditions up at our cabin was much drier and the weather much colder, thus the snow did not get a chance to compact, and I thought a snowmobile would be the way to travel, or at least a pair of snowshoes! The boys didn't think they would have much problem with the Hondas, so they left the Skidoos home! A mistake!

I arrived at the parking spot along the state maintained road before they did, parked my truck, loaded my cooking supplies and sleeping bag into a small plastic sled and while wearing my snowshoes, trudged to the hill below the cabin, and fought my way up the deep snow covered hill to the little twelve by sixteen cabin which overlooked the Mat-Su Valley and the Yenlo Hills far to the west.

Upon reaching the cabin, I noticed an orange extension-cord, which I thought was first a rope someone had used to tie a dog! There was no one who had been given permission to use our cabin, and as I climbed onto the porch and looked at the damaged padlock that was to keep the felons at bay, realized someone had broken into the cabin, and tried to make it their home for a few months the previous summer!

As I opened the door, I soon caught the aroma of "herbs and spices" or "musk type cologne". I could tell it wasn't my brand "Old Spice Aftershave Lotion"! I propped the door open to "air the place out" and could readily see someone or two or three had been using our cabin as if it were their own! I looked back at the porch, and spotted a Coleman cooler that was not ours, and inside was "Potting Soil" and a few small containers for "starting plants". Back I went into the cabin and saw a notebook on the kitchen counter, with notes on how to start plants, speed them to their maturity and how to make the delivery into Wasilla, AK. The notes stated, "Cedar shavings to cover smell. Use Someone else vehicle to go to the grow store. Unload in Garage. ¼ turn A Day (rotating plants for best growth). Never open the truck of the vehicle until the vehicle was inside the garage and the door closed, to keep anyone from seeing the "produce" being delivered!" Whoever wrote the instructions was not a novice! These boys meant business!

A "Tigers 2007 Calendar" shows April, May, and June to have been their busy time of growing, and shows so many days of growing, then "Pay Day". The last page of the four inch by six spiral bound notebook gives an estimate of the "profit". I will copy the notes and the "Estimate Profits" page so you can get a laugh too! Imagine someone bold enough to move into your cabin and turn it into a "Grow Operation"! I am fortunate I did not discover anyone operating this at our cabin. I probably would be in the "Cooler" being furnished "Three Hots and a Cot!" (Three hot meals and a cot to sleep on in the poky). I probably would have had a shoot-out with them!

After seeing all of this, I went to the ladder that led to the sleeping loft and climbed up for a "peek-see". At the entrance end of the loft is a large window that lets in lots of light, and can be opened to allow fresh-air in. Hanging from the ridge-rafter was a "Large Grow Light", its bulb about the size of an eight pound zucchini! The orange extension cord had been threaded over the front door and then up through a hole and into the sleeping loft. I removed the "Grow Light" and sat it out onto the porch. The "Farmers" had left a couple of foam pads for their bed, an old sleeping bag, pair of boots, and a few pair of dirty sox, along with a "Skid-marked" pair of Long-Johns! I went down to my sled and retrieved a new pair of "Monkey-faced cotton gloves" and carefully placed the items of clothing into a fresh, large black garbage bag, sealed the top and dropped it down to the main floor of the cabin. The foam sleeping pad was gingerly dragged over to the opened loft window, and tossed outside, later to be moved to the front yard of the cabin, and with all of the items of clothing and sleeping gear piled neatly, I doused them with "Regular Un-Leaded Gasoline" and then I cautiously "Sanitized" the whole mess by igniting it with a "Bic Lighter", and "Relished" seeing the black smoke rise and disappear into the atmosphere.

Cole gave me a "ring" on my cell phone, and I snow-shoed down to the parking area, and drove out on the main road to meet them. Back at the parking lot, where the Honda four-wheeler had been started and an attempt was made to follow my trail. The Honda settled in the deep snow about twenty feet off the plowed road! Cole and Tim had to wade through the deep snow with places up to their waist, and with no show-shoes! At the cabin, I showed them the "evidence" and we talked about the area.

For many years, no one knew our cabin even existed, much less where it was located. A neighbor who lived about a half mile as the crow flies from our property, had a brown bear on his porch and in an attempt to scare it off, opened the window, poked a .44 Magnum revolver outside and trying to hold it in his left hand (him being

Right-handed) fired the thing, and the with the recoil over-powering him, he dropped the gun onto his porch, out of reach from the window, and not able to go out the front door to retrieve it, as the brown bear was waiting on the porch to get inside and partake of the "Culinary Delights" that were emitted from the stove's oven. As the "Shooter" had a passel of "hairy beasts" ranging from "Mexican Hairless" dog to the large Husky breeds that were now harassing the "Hapless Brown Bear", the bear took flight and vacated the premises.

The "Shooter" wanted to be sure the bear was leaving that part of the Mat-Su Borough, so decided to follow the bear's tracks for awhile. Strapping on his snowshoes, he carried his .30-06 rifle for defense. After following the tracks for quite a while, he heard a "Crashing and Ripping" noise, eased off the trail in the direction of the sound and spotted the brown bear standing at the rear of our cabin, breaking the glass and ripping the aluminum window-jam, in an effort to get into the cabin. As the window was about six feet off the ground, the fat bear was unable to "jump or pull" itself in through the window. The "Shooter" at one point in time thought of shooting the brown bear, but put that idea aside as he did hold an "Expert Shooter" title, and thought he

might only wound the bear, and to be
chewed and scratched up! Up until this
time, the "Shooter" did not know our
cabin existed.   I later met the
"Shooter" and learned he was a
"Professional Chef" and did his baking
and broiling at a near-by lodge.

Cole and Tim and I had a good
night's sleep and I fired-up the
Coleman two burner gas stove and fried
canned Spam, fried potatoes, fried eggs
and a little Chili for covering. This
was a meal that might not "Stick to
your Ribs", but you would later be
reminded you had partaken of it! We
loaded their gear into my small sled
and made our way to the road where they
loaded their truck and "Bid me A-dieu".
While driving out to the main highway,
the "Shooter Chef" stopped them and
said he had seen their truck parked in
my spot, and asked who they might be,
as he knew I was the only person with a
cabin back up on the ridge.   They
informed him they were friends of mine
and I was still up at the cabin. They
also told him of our finding the "Grow
Operation" that had transpired.

The "Shooter" did not have
snowshoes, but trudged up the deep snow
laden trail to the cabin where I was
loading my gear to depart the area! He
told me he had come by my cabin the
summer before and discovered two
fellows "sunning" their "Loco Weed
Flowers" outside my cabin. When he

asked them if I had given them permission to use the cabin, they could not give a good enough answer. He supposedly then told them they would have to leave or he would report them to the Alaska State Troopers. One of the fellows said he thought the cabin was his, as he had purchased a cabin (sight-unseen), and apparently had no idea as to where the cabin was located, but thought this might be the cabin he had purchased. (Now that Real Estate Broker had to be a Dandy). The "Now Lost Landowner" was "Hans" and I believe there was an element of truth somewhere in the wood-pile, just where I have not discovered. I did find a Professional Infusion Pharmacy, Inc. Northway Mall, Anchorage, AK bottle with the name of the recipient "Hans H." in my medicine cabinet, along with other items. I informed my friend the "Shooter Chef", I would shoot anyone I caught growing "dope" in my cabin! Since passing the word along, we have had no further signs of a "Share-crop" operation in the cabin. I did call the Alaska State Troopers while Cole and Tim were with me at the cabin, and informed the Troopers of the operation, and they gave me the number of the "Drug Enforcement Department". While the Troopers were on the phone, I asked them, "Do you want me to shoot them light or shoot them heavy?" The phone was as though it were "Dead". I asked the same question, "Do you want me to shoot them light or shoot them heavy?" Nothing! The question was asked three times, and I got no response. I said, "Well, I guess I'll have to use my own judgment!"

A short while before I had driven up to the cabin to have a "Real Estate Open House", there was an article in the newspaper reporting a "Drug Deal Gone Bad" that took place just a few blocks from where we park our vehicle on the gravel road. One of the players was shot and killed. The gun smoke has since cleared!

The old saying, "Time Heals All Wounds" may have an element of truth to it, as the area has taken on a more "wholesome atmosphere". I even met a new neighbor building near our parking area who actually had worked for a living, on a real job, not just growing and distributing illegal narcotics! This fellow had worked long enough to retire doing honest work! Not long after meeting this new neighbor, I met another man and his wife who live in the next development, and he works on the North Slope, and was friends with many of my old friends from Anchorage, and these were good and honest people who actually go to work each day and pay taxes and put in an effort for their subsistence! Things are positively looking up!

"WELDER'S FLASH" AT THE KITTY CAT CLUB!

Thelma, an old friend from the "Homestead Days on Halbouty Road, North Kenai" was visiting with us at our Lower Hillside home in Anchorage, and we were having a grand old time! In the old days, she was known as "One Gear Thelma" as she never learned the meaning of "synchronize", and usually grounded a pound or two of transmission gears when shifting on the move! Her preferred method was to step on the clutch, shift into Low Gear, rev the engine to the red line, and pop the clutch! The gravel would fly! 'Tis a wonder she didn't break the window glass on the little lean-to, the only grace was, the windows were on the other side of the building! Thelma and husband Howard, who worked for the Alaska Railroad as a crane operator had homesteaded in the area of a beautiful lake they named "Barbara Lake". He wanted to "retire" a few years earlier, but she had talked him into working just a few more years, so their retirement check would be more attractive! With the "Time Clock Punched for the Last Time", Howard "Pulled the Pin" and they purchased a beautiful motor home, with plans of now traveling and enjoying life!

That was not to be! Very soon after Howard purchased the motor home, he was diagnosed with leukemia, and only lasted a few months! The "Fickle Finger of Fate" had played a terrible trick on them! Now, Thelma resided alone in their longtime home in Spenard. Sharon and I tried to visit her when possible, and today was one of the enjoyable days we were able to spend together. I had driven to Spenard and brought her to our home for lunch and an afternoon's visit. We were feasting on "Smoked King Salmon" bellies, moose summer sausage and Polish sausage, and crackers, all washed down with hot coffee or hot black tea with liberal amounts of "Pure Cane Sugar From Hawaii"! I was sitting in my high back rocking chair and was putting the miles on it, rocking back and forth.

About that time, the phone rang, and it was an emergency water pump repair call, as my wife and I owned a Water Well Drilling and Service Company. The day was a Saturday, and if I postponed the service call to Monday, the business would have to be shut down until then. As our work had been slow, I was game for the "Over Time Work". The caller, an owner-bartender opted to pay the "Higher Time Rate", so I informed my wife and Thelma, I would be back as soon as possible! Just save some of the summer sausage for me! And a few Ritz crackers!

I drove my Pump Service Truck to the Old Seward Highway, and soon turned in to the gravel parking lot littered with potholes standing with water, as it was raining. Ahead was the old building with the bright lights proclaiming this was the "Kit Cat Club", a notorious strip-joint hangout of the "Hells Angels", and a few other rough fellows! The outside reminded me of an old weathered, unpainted plywood sided building you might see at an abandoned military base along the Aleutian Chain!

I put on my tool belt and carried an electrical testing machine for trouble shooting. When I walked through the door, my eyes were greeted by the flashy bright colored lights, the very dirty floor, tables and chairs in the main room and to the side were two customers perched on barstools at the bar, and wearing leather motorcycle pants and black "Hells Angels" leather vests. Almost everyone in the establishment glanced my way and made a quick inspection, and then their attention was back to their drinks!

The bartender came over to introduce himself and I asked what had happened? "Well, it seems the water flow just quit!" I asked where the water tank and control box was located, he led me toward the stage, and up onto it and we walked to an opening with a thin curtain that hid the "dressing

245

room" where the water tank and controls were located. It was a slack time between performances, so the dressing room was unoccupied. There was no sheetrock on the wall where the control box was located, and the wiring was exposed, dangling loose, and covered with dusty spider webs. This would not pass an Electrical Building Inspection! I quickly checked the controls and said, "I believe the water pump has died!" I then asked, "Where is the well located? I'll have to back my pump service truck next to it to pull the pump."

"You can't back the truck next to the well! The well is located under the main dance floor, just in front of the stage where the "Mares" perform!" I said, "You mean I'm going to have to pull the submersible pump and pipe by hand?" His answer was, "Yes, and you'll have to do it by yourself, as I have a 'Bad Back' and can't lift over twenty five pounds!" (Probably twenty pounds of $50.00's and $100.00 bills!)

We jumped down from the stage and moved the unoccupied tables back against the wall, trying not to disturb the other patrons, as the bartender did not want to "slow their drinking". I told him to get a broom or a shovel and remove the mud and gravel off this throw rug before we move it. With it out of the way, I pried the plywood hatch up enough to grab hold of it and pushed it aside. I had to climb into the opening and stand on the ground with the floor joists at my waist! This was going to be a "Doozy!" Little did I know what was in store!

I walked to my service truck, unlocked the tool cabinets, chose the needed hand tools and clamps to secure the water pump drop pipe during the operation, and walked back into the room, now the music had picked up and there was activity on the stage! The opening in the floor required me to face the stage during the pump removal and replacement! I had to pull my baseball cap down low on my eye brow to avoid the distractions. The "Mares" were kicking and frolicking and putting on a show on the stage!

I finally got the old pump removed, and had been correct. The unit had burned out and was later discarded. During the installation of the pump, on stage was a "Matched Pair of Oriental Mares", as the bartender called them, flashing their buttocks and appendages. At one point of this operation, I had to raise my head and reach for a pipe wrench lying near the opening on the floor. The dancers apparently were doing their famous "Around The World Maneuver" and when I glanced up, they were approaching the "High Noon" position of the arch! I saw something "FLASH!"

"BOOM!" At that moment I am sure I got a "Welder's Flash!" My eyes were burning! I finally completed the installation, and received my pay check and got out of there! That was my first and last time ever at the Kit Cat Club!

I had been the Hero, by repairing the water system and allowing the "Mares to Perform" and the "Show To Go On", and the bartender to keep the "Green Backs" flowing into his coffer! But I knew if ever I had to return for service work on the water system, I'd definitely need "Dark, Dark Glasses" or a "Welder's Hood" to protect my eyes!

An Evening with Earl and Florence
At Their Daniels Lake Cabin

The Sun had long retired from duty, taking a well earned rest, having warmed the gentle blueberry scattered slope next to the lake, chased the dew from the foliage, forced the mist from the lake, and blanketed the earth with warmth. The grass and leaves of the trees and bushes had dried, soaked up the sun's rays for energy, and were now at peace. And now the Moon possessed the night. A globe-less Coleman double burner lantern hanging from a nail driven into the ten inch log rafter above the small table, hissed, sometime spitted and flickered, calling for attention for more air to be pumped into the fuel tank, as the harsh light held the darkness at bay. Over in the center of the room, a six inch steel blue stove pipe that was stained with creosote which had bled from its' joint, due to the use of the green birch firewood, radiated heat. The pipe was lost from view as it disappeared upward through a metal stove pipe jack that was mounted in the tongue and groove pine plank ceiling. This pipe climbed upward, through the gray galvanized roof jack, and stood like a sentinel at attention on the roof, as if watching the movements of the pail butter colored moon. Connected to the lower portion of the pipe, the oval shaped body of the chrome trimmed Ashley Airtight Wood Stove with its short, slightly curved, sturdy legs resting on a brown colored metal mat to keep the heat from charring the wood floor, radiated the comforting warmth around the room, and resting on its' top, sat a tannin stained silver colored tea pot, with a curved neck like a young swan, hissing as it simmered, putting moisture into the room. Around the table we gathered, occasionally pouring more steaming water onto the tea bags in our cups, and stirred sugar into the Lipton black tea, as we read from the old Field and Stream magazines and the book, "Alaska-Yukon Trophies/ Won and Lost".

Over on the small kitchen counter, next to the white enamel sink with a cast-iron pitcher pump, sat a can of Darigold Sweet Cream Butter, its' key still attached to the can, signifying it was un-opened. A jar of homemade strawberry jam fresh from the cupboard and with the Mason lid remaining sealed stood at the ready to satisfy the "sweet-tooth" desire of the inhabitants of the wilderness cabin. Between the kitchen counter and the table, sat a now idle four burner, white Dixie brand propane stove with its' oven door slightly ajar as it cooled, the oven's flame now hushed. On an old buff-brown colored wooden cutting board, scarred from duties past, a freshly baked loaf of Sourdough bread cooled, waiting to be dissected with the long, thin razor sharp, steel blade of the LL Bean butcher knife. Silence gripped the cabin as the inhabitants immersed themselves into the stories they read, and a "Who, Who, Whooooo are you" was heard from the owl outside that hunted the moon lit landscape, and the dark shadowed woods for its' supper.

Late into the night we sat and read, engulfed in the intriguing stories, of lives filled with adventure. The Field and Stream magazines stacked onto the table contained the series of articles written by Russell Annabel, entitled "Adventure Is My Business". Also being read was a book entitled, "Alaskan – Yukon Trophies Won and Lost" by G.O. Young, published by Standard Publications, Incorporated, Huntington, West Virginia, 1947. This book later left Earl's & Florence's cabin when Earl passed away. It was given to a dear friend Lance Ware, whose family had homesteaded on the north end on of Daniels Lake in the late 1950's. After Sharon and I purchased the Daniels cabin in 1993, and moved back to the north Kenai area in 1994, Lance brought the book over to the cabin and presented it to me as gift, "Saying it belonged at its home in the cabin." At that time the book was out of print,

and the copies were valued at about
$1,200.00 each. Praise the Lord! A
true friend indeed!

A Side Note: If you were at Earl and
Florence's cabin and the batteries were
good in the Zenith Trans-Oceanic radio,
and the time was early-evening, you had
better mind your P's and Q's and limit
your conversation when Ruben Gaines'
program, "Conversation Unlimited" came
on. We always listened attentively as
he spoke of "Six-Toed Mordecai", and
about the Lake Ness type Monster of
Iliamna Lake that rose from the deep
and tipped over the red boat! And we
were treated with many other stories of
the Alaskan Bush.
The Moral of Ruben Gaines' story: Never
paint your boat red!

I've tried not to "bore" you too much, and have more true tales coming. I hope not all of the "Good Camps" are behind us! There are still a few hot coals in the fire pit. Toss some of the dry willow and spruce branches on, and "Take off your Fedora and Fan the Fire!" We'll stir the campfire and put on a fresh pot of coffee with that clean and cold mountain stream water and get ready for another session!

Remember, "When there's Lead In the Air, there is Danger About!

Keep the Campfire Burning!

Alaska Vern
"The Bishop Creek Trapper"